Praise for *The B*

'Dannielle Miller is the teen girl whisperer.'

Fran Simpson, teacher and mother of a teen

'Dannielle Miller's book is a must-read for all parents of teenage girls. The first thing that literally thumped me in the chest when reading this book was a total awareness and awakening of what is happening to our teenage girls. At a deep level, it resonated with me. The information is real, pertinent and totally relevant.

'Great work, Dannielle. Thank you for awakening me. Thank you for snapping me to attention and making me want to become a greater part of the solution.'

Karen, mother of a teen girl

'This is the book we have been waiting for. It includes the most up-to-date research and finally gives parents positive, sensible strategies they can easily apply.'

Dr Michele Beale, general practitioner
and stress management specialist

the butterfly effect

effect

a positive new approach to raising
happy, confident teen girls

Dannielle Miller, B.Ed

BANTAM

SYDNEY AUCKLAND TORONTO NEW YORK LONDON

A Bantam book
Published by Random House Australia Pty Ltd
Level 3, 100 Pacific Highway, North Sydney NSW 2060
www.randomhouse.com.au

First published by Doubleday in 2009

Addresses for companies within the Random House Group
can be found at www.randomhouse.com.au/offices

National Library of Australia
Cataloguing-in-Publication Entry

Miller, Dannielle
The butterfly effect.

ISBN 978 1 86471 105 9 (pbk).

Parenting.
Parenting and teenager.
Teenage girls.

649.125

Cover design by Ciara Fulcher
Cover image courtesy Shutterstock
Typeset in 12/17 pt Sabon Roman by Post Pre-press Group, Australia
Printed in Australia by Griffin Press, an accredited ISO AS/NZS 14001:2004
Environmental Management System printer

Random House Australia uses papers that are natural, renewable and
recyclable products and made from wood grown in sustainable forests.
The logging and manufacturing processes are expected to conform
to the environmental regulations of the country of origin.

For Teyah and Kye.

xxx

Contents

Foreword

❧

Not all is well in teenage girl world. Research statistics portray an alarming story of increasing self-harm, body image problems and eating disorders, binge drinking and depression. Dannielle Miller is not the first person to call attention to these issues, to the phenomenon of girls' lives sometimes falling apart at the very threshold of woman-hood. But in this candid and thought-provoking book, written with passion and conviction, she offers not only insight into adolescent girls as interesting *works in progress*, but also provides encouragement, solace and solution. She reminds us, too, I am pleased to say, that we (their mothers *and* fathers) are also works in progress.

Dannielle Miller approaches the realities, challenges and opportunities facing adolescent girls from a uniquely per-sonal perspective – as someone who has herself known pain, suffering and rejection (and risen above it), and as someone who has accessed the inner lives, concerns and aspirations of many thousands of young women.

Our current obsession with the achievement of air-brushed perfection is not good for our daughters. Rather, we need to be ourselves and to foster this novel idea in our offspring. This book is timely, its contemporary information enlightening and empowering. It enables us to tune into what's currently happening in the unfolding lives of girls – how they think and learn, how they cope (or don't) with conflict with friends, how they deal with peer and societal pressure to be thin, to be sexually active, to drink and smoke.

The Butterfly Effect unpacks the nature of the relationship between mothers and their teenage daughters. With warmth and wisdom, it sketches out a blueprint for women, to make this journey more manageable. It promotes empathy and understanding, first and foremost, and then spells out what to do – mostly simple things and a shared approach that involves 'sorting out this mess alongside your daughter'. In reading this book (as a health professional, father and grandfather), I found myself frequently thinking, 'Yes – this is good, this needs to be said, this is exactly what girls need their mothers to know, reflect upon and respond to.' I also felt a prickly discomfort related to unfortunate truths – gender inequity in the workplace, the sexualisation of children, commercial exploitation of teenagers through advertising. These are matters, boldly addressed here, that should concern us all, women and men alike.

Above all, *The Butterfly Effect* dispels the widely held notion, when it comes to our teenage daughters, that it's all too hard. It provides a sense of hope, suggests we pause and think about *why* we might be pushing our daughters away – when they so desperately want us to be there – and asks us to capture the joyfulness that is part of being a young woman even when it's temporarily hidden from view.

Clinical Professor David Bennett AO FRACP FSAM, Head, NSW Centre for the Advancement of Adolescent Health, The Children's Hospital at Westmead; President, Association for the Wellbeing of Children in Healthcare; and co-author (with Leanne Rowe and Bruce Tonge) of *I Just Want You to be Happy* (Allen & Unwin, 2009)

Author's Note

A great deal of research on the issues affecting teen girls' lives has been conducted by psychologists, sociologists, healthcare professionals and other experts. Throughout this book I have considered their data, which has been published in various professional journals and research papers. I am focused on keeping up to date with the latest statistics because they give us a measurable insight into what is happening in girl world.

I also know that the raw numbers do not tell the whole story. They do not always tell us how girls feel about themselves, their world and their place in it. So in addition to statistics and expert opinion, I have also collated the more detailed and personal information you can really only get by taking the time to sit down and discuss the issues with teen girls. I have gathered this research formally and informally over the many years I have worked with young people as a teacher, as a coordinator for students at risk and as the co-founder and CEO of Enlighten Education.

The girls I listened to

In my role with Enlighten Education, I have had the opportunity to work with thousands of teenage girls across Australia. In New South Wales, where I am based, I personally work with over 4,000 teenage girls in a year.

Listening and talking with girls is my life's work.

I lead workshops for groups of teen girls that focus on issues relevant to them and that provide the opportunity for authentic, constructive conversations on friendships, body image, the media's portrayal of girls and women, the sexualisation and objectification of girls and women, and girls' career aspirations – the very issues discussed in this book. Each course runs for a half or full day. I always debrief afterwards by recording my observations and the insights I gain.

I do, therefore, believe that through my work I get a broad overview on what girls think about issues that really matter to them. Just as importantly, I get to observe firsthand how they feel about being girls and how they act around each other. My viewpoint is relatively unique in that I am not perceived by them as a teacher or other type of authority figure. By opening myself up to the girls and quickly establishing a sense of intimacy and connection through telling my own personal stories, I am able to almost immediately establish trust. The courses are held on the girls' own turf, at school; the conversations are organic; and I can observe not only the ways they respond to the topics but also to one another.

I am convinced that what I see, hear and feel is absolutely authentic.

During the course of my work, girls often seek me out for one-on-one conversations; and I frequently receive letters, emails and postcards from them. Girls are craving women who will hear them. The correspondence I receive from teen girls has also shaped my insights and this book.

Additionally, while writing this book, I have gone back to interview in more depth girls I have met who struck me as particularly interesting or perceptive; I have shared their thoughts throughout these pages.

Enlighten Education works with girls from a wide variety of backgrounds. I have presented in schools for students with significant behaviour issues. (And how I love the honesty of these girls. One told me as she came in to my session, 'You've got five minutes. If I think you're shit, I am leaving.') I have worked with girls in the most exclusive schools, with harbour views; girls in remote rural areas; girls in selective schools. I have accessed a far broader range of teenage girls than many researchers could ever have access to.

The experts I listened to

I have developed a wonderful rapport with many teachers, principals and experts on girls' and women's issues and adolescent mental health. I am indebted to them for the many conversations we have had, and to the readings and research that we have shared. Some of their beliefs and observations are included in this book, and it is richer for their contributions.

The mothers I listened to

In recent years, I have run night-time workshops for parents of teen girls. I was astonished at first by just how desperate the mothers were to talk about how they felt as women: they believed that many of the issues I spoke about were relevant to their lives, too. Their bravery was inspiring; they had the courage to admit that they were struggling to help their daughters navigate an increasingly problematic world.

These women did not want to merely survive their daughters' adolescence, nor did they want to continue feeling that, as women, they were 'not enough': not skinny enough, not beautiful enough, not popular enough, not successful enough.

These women wanted to make things right for their daughters and for themselves.

I heard their voices, too.

1

Introducing the Butterfly Effect

~

Bratz™, Britney™ and Bacardi Breezers™

Girls are excelling in all kinds of ways – academically, socially and on the sporting field to name a few – but underneath that façade of success, our girls are in trouble. While they may appear to be coping with all that life throws at them, behind closed doors many are silently imploding. Teenage girls exist in a world of peer pressure and unrealistic self-expectations, a world subtly skewed by the insidious marketing hype of popular brands such as Bratz, Britney and Bacardi Breezers. And it is poisoning them at a most vulnerable age.

The statistics show there is much to be alarmed by. A

quarter of teenage girls surveyed in Australia say they would get plastic surgery if they could. Among 15-year-old girls, almost seven in ten are on a diet, and of these, 8 per cent are severely dieting. Peer pressure is a cause of pain for many, with six in ten girls saying they have been teased about their appearance.

Seven out of ten teenage girls engage in binge drinking – consuming five or more alcoholic drinks on one occasion – and almost one in five do so on a weekly basis. An alarming 12 per cent of girls report drinking harmful levels of alcohol – more than five standard drinks on any one day – and twice the number of teenage girls use drugs, compared with boys.

Pressure at school is also an issue, with nearly two out of three girls questioned in an Australian survey saying they feel stressed about their studies.

As many as one in ten teenage girls self-harm. Male suicide rates remain considerably higher than female suicide rates, but there is evidence to suggest that women, particularly those under twenty-five, *attempt* suicide and commit self-harm at a higher rate than men. It is estimated that for each female suicide, there are 150 to 300 acts of self-harm performed by females.

It seems that unprotected sex is resulting in unwanted outcomes for some. Sexually transmitted diseases are on the increase among young people. It has been estimated that as many as 28 per cent of teenagers have chlamydia. In Australia, pregnancy termination, or abortion, is the second-most common hospital procedure for females aged 12 to 24 years.

All of this troubles me. Deeply. For I love children. More than I ever thought I could – and not just my own children. The love and the empathy I have for children seem at times so very large and hard to contain. It arrived suddenly and unexpectedly into my life. Certainly it was not there in my early years as a high school teacher. Nor was it present after the birth of my first child, Teyah Rose. I loved her, but not *every child*. Rather, this love snuck up on me during my years as a senior educator working with students at risk.

In 1999, I founded The Lighthouse Project, a highly successful mentoring program for young people at risk of leaving school early. As coordinator of the program until 2004, one of the many invaluable lessons I learnt was that even teenagers who deliberately set out to be unlovable *crave* love – in fact, their need for affection and connection can be particularly urgent.

It was these troubled young people who finally, unequivocally, won my heart. They demanded authenticity, passion and an adult willing to fight for them, so I became that person.

The knowledge that teenage girls are in crisis also troubles me for the simple fact that I am a woman who believes in women's rights. It would be seductively easy to become complacent: women have the right to vote; there are now laws against sexual discrimination; we have made inroads into higher education, politics, business . . .

Yet we have not managed to make much more than a crack in our own bathroom mirrors, our self-imposed glass ceilings. And I am left wondering how we can expect the next generation of women – our girls – to step up and change the world when they, too, are preoccupied with wanting to change themselves, obsessed with achieving air-brushed perfection.

While boys have it tough and are battling their own demons, I realised that it was the battle for the hearts and minds of girls that I was compelled to take on. I decided to change my career in 2002 and established Enlighten Education, an Australian company that works in schools nationally and internationally. We offer girls programs that address the toxic messages they are fed and ensure these are countered with messages of strength and resilience.

I loved how today was really open and special and how the true piece of everyone came out, because it means a lot to me to know I am not alone. You taught me to be my true self and to be happy and to love, and never to be someone who just makes other people happy.

Kim, 14

I learnt we can be self-destructive and how much there is we can do to build ourselves and those around us up. The media is playing a big part in this problem . . . we are all beautiful.

Claire, 16

I thought it would be one of those cheesy 'You've got to boost your self-esteem' programs but it wasn't. I liked the bit where we realised how fake everything out there really is; I liked how GENUINE this was. You taught me there are many girls just like me, that there are women out there who take the time and care about us, and that all of us are special.

Epitna, 15

So, in my years immersed in field research – working with thousands of teenage girls, their teachers and their parents – what have I learnt? What has made our daughters so angry? So sad? So worried? And more importantly, *how can we all make it okay from now on*? These are the questions that occupy me both in my role within Enlighten and as a mother of a ten-year-old girl: she is just about to hit the 'puberty blues'. It is these questions that I seek to address in this book.

Botox, body image and binge drinking

The search for solutions to the problems our girls face haunts many mothers. While it haunts fathers, too, ultimately I believe fixing this mess is women's business, for we are the ones who show girls every day how to wear the label 'woman'. And we do not always wear this label as a badge of honour.

The reality is, many women are equally unhappy. Studies have shown that while up to 68 per cent of teenage girls think they are less beautiful than the average girl, 84 per cent of women over the age of 40 think they are less beautiful than the average woman. A 2008 *Australian Women's Weekly* survey of 15,000 women found that only one in six were happy with their weight, one in five had such a poor body image they avoided mirrors and almost half would have cosmetic surgery if they could afford it. Binge drinking appeared to be rife, too. A third of the women surveyed drank too much and one in five suspected she had a drinking problem.

Many of us tell our daughters they do not need to change in order to be beautiful, while we rush for Botox. We tell them inner beauty counts, while we devour magazines that tell us beauty is really only about air-brushed perfection after all. If even the grown-ups are struggling, is it any wonder that our daughters are? Girls cannot be what they cannot see.

It seems that in many significant ways we are far more like our daughters than we are different from them. How desperately sad.

But this recognition of sameness is also full of possibility. If we accept that the issues we need to work on affect all girls and women, then we have the opportunity to sort this mess out *alongside our daughters*. We no longer need to maintain the 'Mother knows best' façade and try to 'fix' everything for them. Or worse still, rage at their unhealthy behaviours, which really only parallel our own – how teen girls hate hypocrisy!

A deeper connection with our daughters

We can join our daughters and work together on something greater; together we can find new connections and deeper mutual understanding. In this book, I want to challenge you to do just that: to form a new connection with your daughter, niece, stepdaughter – with all the young women close to you – and work with them to bring about change. Don't aim merely to 'survive' girls' adolescence, as some other parenting books will encourage you to do. Let's aim for something far more mutually respectful and rewarding.

If you are currently caught up in screaming fights or in passive-aggressive girl hell – and yes, I do acknowledge that teen girls are gifted at turning their anger on those who are closest – I can see why books that promise survival might appeal. But isn't the old 'Mothers and daughters just do not get along; teen girls are hell' argument just a little clichéd? It is certainly disrespectful to both parties.

If you, like many of us, have been fed that oppositional, woman-pitted-against-woman approach for years, my invitation to begin a more empathetic journey of parenting through self-discovery may seem too simplistic. Or, if you are caught up in conflict with your teen girl right now, it may seem unobtainable. Let me assure you, I am not setting out to make mothers feel any more inadequate than they may feel already. Girls may do seething anger well, but women do guilt better; we're gifted at blaming ourselves for everything that goes wrong.

I am not one of the 'Mummy Police', the smug parenting experts who leave me feeling like I am doing everything wrong. I found myself particularly susceptible to them in my early days as a mother. I spent my time with my new daughter, Teyah, sleep deprived and bewildered by what I was supposed to do with this new and oh-so-perfect creature. I thought I had to be the perfect mother; she deserved nothing less. Those were desperate days spent madly reading every book I could find – and becoming even more confused as one only seemed to contradict the next. In the end it was

Baby Love, by Australian Robin Barker, that resonated with me. Why? Because she emphasised the need for following one's instincts, and love was put at the forefront, right there in the title. Isn't that what it is supposed to be about, after all? Teyah didn't need a perfect mother; she needed a happy, confident, loving one.

Your teenage daughter does not need perfection, either. It may surprise you to know that out of the many thousands of young people who have crossed my path, including those from very troubled backgrounds, very few have ever questioned their parents' skills or said they wished their mothers were better at parenting, or were thinner, more beautiful, more successful. Rather, they have told me they want more time, more love, more empathy and more happiness.

I believe the key is empathy. Instead of viewing adolescence as a stage in which fights between mothers and daughters are inevitable, try viewing it as a stage when a new connection can be found and a new level in your relationship reached. And empathy should be easy. Her pain may be your pain. Her struggles may be your struggles.

Make no mistake, I am not suggesting you stop parenting and become your daughter's new 'bestie'. The other thing that young people consistently tell me they want more of from their parents is boundaries. Your daughter needs to see what a strong, confident, healthy woman looks like, how she copes with mistakes and failures, how she sets boundaries, and how she demands to be treated, both within the home and by society as a whole. If you won't show her, who will?

In recent years a number of books have come out on the plight of teen girls in our hyper-sexual, commercialised and media-saturated culture. These books are valuable because they provide a real insight into teen-girl world – but they risk leaving us in a state of despair, feeling that it's all too hard to make changes in our daughters' lives. It's not! Offered here are practical steps we can take to work towards making things better.

The best thing mothers can do is just be there. Just be reliable. We need to know that there is someone who loves us and who will listen and is on our side, as it often feels like no one else is on our side. My mum doesn't have to fix my problems, as sometimes she can't fix them – but she is great at just really hearing me talk about them and getting them all out of my system.

Lucy, 16

Mothers need to demonstrate that they are strong women who know their strengths and weaknesses and can live with both, irrespective of what others might think. It is a tall order but we can do it.

Amelia Toffoli, Principal, St Brigid's Girls School, WA

Harnessing the butterfly effect

The idea of the butterfly effect comes from the science of chaos theory. It suggests that everything in this world is interconnected, to the extent that the beating of a butterfly's wings in one part of the world may ultimately contribute to a tornado happening in another part of the world. Small changes can make a huge difference. My hope is that you may harness the butterfly effect in your relationship with your daughter by being conscious that your actions and words – even ones that seem trivial – have a big influence on your daughter, just as her peers and the media influence her.

There is another aspect of the butterfly that I believe we could all embrace and learn from: its amazing life cycle. Maya Angelou wrote, 'We delight in the beauty of the butterfly, but rarely admit the changes it has gone through to achieve that beauty.' This is a message that speaks to both mother and daughter. Teen girls go through a period of rapid and at times difficult change; at the same time, mothers may find themselves struggling with similar issues to their daughters. This book is an open invitation to mothers to undergo that same gradual unfolding as the butterfly, along with our daughters.

Just as I do when I work with young girls, in this book I shall endeavour to appeal to your head, hand and heart.

For your head, I provide relevant research and statistics.

For your hand, there are practical things you can do right now, as well as changes you can make in the long term, to help you and your daughter. At the end of each of the next chapters you will find action plans and affirmations. Each action plan provides hands-on advice to help you work with your daughter to face the issues described in that chapter. The affirmations are short, positive statements that you and your daughter can use to bolster your strength or chart a new course in your lives. Some people find it helpful to repeat an affirmation when they wake each morning; others turn to them when the going gets tough. Some like to write affirmations down and pin them up around the house, or put them in their diary or journal.

At the end of the book, you will find appendices that provide you and your daughter with practical activities you can do individually or together. I have used all of these with teen girls and their mothers and have had very positive feedback about them.

Most importantly, in this book I appeal to your heart, by sharing my stories and those of the girls I have met along the way. I hope that the advice makes intuitive, emotional sense to you, as I believe that is the only kind of advice anyone should follow.

Always at the centre of my approach is love and laughter – and there is nothing soft or airy-fairy about this. Research clearly indicates that building positive emotions and healthy connections with other people makes us feel far healthier and more joyful. There is also good evidence that we need to be warmer and more nurturing, but firmer, with our teenagers.

Tailoring the butterfly effect to your daughter

In *The Butterfly Effect*, I have not made the common parenting-book distinction between early, middle and late adolescence, for I believe the issues I am discussing may have an impact on girls right across all three stages.

I originally designed Enlighten Education's programs specifically for high school girls, not envisaging a demand for our work in primary schools. Surely 11-year-old girls were not yet doubting themselves and playing the 'compare and despair' game? It soon became apparent that, yes, the very same issues were also relevant for girls in the late primary school years. 'We are seeing girls as young as ten suffering from crippling self-doubt, engaging in bullying based on appearances, at risk of developing fully blown eating disorders,' explains Fran Simpson, religious education coordinator at St John Vianney's Primary School, in Wollongong. 'And even those girls who are still enjoying their childhood and are not yet struggling to develop an identity as young women need to hear these messages, too, for if we can give our little girls age-appropriate information now, then perhaps we can vaccinate them against some of the more toxic elements of popular culture. We want to be proactive rather than reactive; why wait until our girls are in high school to pick up the pieces?'

On the flip side, adults sometimes underestimate the guidance that older teens need. I have worked with 15-year-old girls who still do not know how to make friends or get organised at school, both skills that adults assume girls have already mastered in early adolescence.

Every girl is unique; what counts is not so much your daughter's chronological age but her stage of development. In many cases, the advice I offer in this book will be suitable for your daughter as it is, but in other instances you may want to adapt it to suit her. You know her best.

As a general rule, younger girls tend to be concrete thinkers, which means they respond best when given actual examples and specific steps that they can immediately make. They may need encouragement to begin forming and verbalising their own thoughts on how issues affect them. As girls develop the ability to be more abstract in their thinking, they become able to consider hypotheticals. Their opinions and outlooks broaden; they consider the wider implications of their actions; and they become better able to form future goals. They may also enjoy questioning and challenging other people's opinions.

My aim in writing this book has been to make my advice and reflections relevant to girls and women of all ages so I hope that you, too, will be open to the suggestions here. It is never too late to change your outlook or develop a new internal dialogue.

Finally, I must admit at times to feeling almost paralysed by the enormity of writing a book on parenting. Doesn't it imply I must consider myself an expert on being a parent? I don't. I just do the best I can on any given day. I am not an all-seeing, all-knowing expert, nor am I an academic. I am a teacher, a practitioner, a mother, a woman. The aim of this book is to share my understanding of teen girls, my insights, my empathy and the strategies I have tried and that I know work.

But enough talk, let's begin.

2

The Battle Within

⤬

A young English girl who calls herself 'Mememolly' started a phenomenon on YouTube when she posted 'something of an apologetic love letter' to her body in 2007. She listed parts of her body – her feet, arms, ears, eyes – and talked about why she appreciated them. A flood of people responded by posting their own video responses in which they told the world how they feel about their bodies.

Inspired by them, on the morning that I turned 38, I sat down and wrote my own letter of thanks to my body:

Dear body,

I am really happy with the way we are growing old together.

Thanks, feet, for being so pretty. I love the way your nails look when they are painted. I haven't always treated you so well, though. I have stopped wearing killer heels quite so often, but hey, we both know the damage is done.

Thanks, legs. You are fabulous; you're so long and you rarely change shape, even when I eat loads of junky foods. You have made me feel glamorous on many occasions.

Belly – what can I say? You are a podgy, bloated little thing, aren't you? I have tried exercising you, sucking you in and constraining you in special 'Bridget Jones' style bloomers – but you just will not be denied.

Breasts – you will not be denied, either, but you are lovely. You make me feel so feminine. And you fed both my children; that was truly amazing. I will be forever grateful.

Arms. My special body parts. Lefty – you are a bit of a non-event really, aren't you? I don't write with you and you are quite nondescript. But righty – yes, you have tales to tell. I love your burn scars now. Really. I do. You make me strong, unique and show the world I am a girl with a history of bravery. I am sorry that I hid you for so many years when I was young, but I just hadn't learnt how to deal with something so large. We both had to grow into the tight, twisted and melted flesh.

Face – you are just fine. Elegantly shaped eyebrows, a few wrinkles that show I have lived, laughed and worried.

Hair – I am sorry I bleach you. You do well to hang in there – but I do treat you to great shampoos and head rubs from my girlfriends.

Thanks, body, for getting me this far. You are so resilient and so strong. You rarely get sick and you can withstand great pain. You are an Amazon's body.

Happy Birthday. xxxx

Scarred and scared

When I was two years old, I was badly burnt. I received third-degree burns all down my right arm and neck. As is often the case with burn victims, I also suffered two major secondary infections, German measles and the potentially life-threatening golden staph.

My great-grandmother burnt me; she poured hot cooking oil down on me as I sat watching breakfast being prepared. As a small girl, I was always told this was an accident, yet I questioned why no one ever spoke of this woman again, let alone saw her. Why hadn't we forgiven her? I wondered. After all, accidents do happen. It was only when I was older that the truth emerged. Great Grandma had been unstable and had shown signs of violence towards my beloved grandmother when she was a small girl, too. Everyone felt instinctively that she had burnt me deliberately.

I don't remember whether it was done to me deliberately; and ultimately, as it cannot be undone, I have chosen not to focus on that question. It happened.

What do I remember? I remember my grandmother's face as she came through the doorway in response to my screams. I recall thinking I must be very badly hurt as she looked stricken. I remember my doctor, too. As I was hospitalised for almost six months, he became a central figure in my life. He was kind, gentle and doting. I was his special girl. Heaven help any nurse who dared keep me waiting! I remember gifts, in particular books. Perhaps this was the start of my love affair with words. I loved being read to. I escaped pain and boredom through tales of princesses with power and adventures of other little girls who faced great dangers and emerged triumphant.

I soothed myself with words, too. I could not yet read, of course, but I would talk to myself when frightened, repeating over and over the mantra 'You'll be okay, you'll be all right.' It was my secret spell and I would cast it to give me strength.

How fortunate that these are my memories: of being loved, spoilt, protected and strong.

For my family, other, darker memories remain as well. Memories of me writhing in pain as my dressings were changed, of being told that my arm would need to be amputated, of being advised that I would need yet another skin graft, of being told time and time again that I would not live.

But live I did. And I kept my arm. With its red, raised, twisted flesh, it looked different to the arms of my friends. There was a flap of skin near my elbow that was taut when my arm was stretched out and hung loose when my arm was bent. Yet as a small child these differences did not concern me – I was so much more than my body!

I was a busy, bossy little girl. I had a beloved younger sister to organise, lollies to eat, Barbies to collect and, once school started, more books to devour. In childhood, my body was merely an instrument to carry me from one adventure to the next. When I wanted to join my friends at the beach, I just had Mum cut the toes out of one of my father's socks and popped that on to protect my arm from the sun. Problem solved!

Around the time I turned ten, things definitely changed. I started noticing boys. And I started noticing the girls the boys noticed. At school, the boys preferred the alpha girls: popular, pretty, often good at sport. I was a pretty enough girl and had a few close friends, but as I was more interested in reading than netball, I was definitely not alpha material. It wasn't just at school that I received messages about what defined beauty and sexual attractiveness. My Barbies, *Charlie's Angels*, ABBA – all of them taught me that to be a desired woman, I would need to be thin, beautiful and immaculately groomed. No scars allowed.

I entered adolescence and, like most girls, began a new internal conversation. I was no longer casting spells to heal myself. Instead, I was engaging in darker, self-destructive thoughts and telling myself that I was not enough. Not pretty enough, not thin enough, not popular enough. My feelings of inadequacy due to my scarring became quite overwhelming; I was still bright and ambitious but my main preoccupation was how best I could hide my scars from the world.

I hid. I hid my arm. I wore skivvies underneath my summer uniform, wore jumpers all year round. I avoided pools and beaches. My arm no longer seemed small; it seemed enormous. A huge, horrible, disfigured limb I would be forced to drag through what had been my oh-so-promising life.

Yes, teenage girls are good at drama.

I vividly recall my daydreams at age 15 about what my

life would be like if I had not been burnt. I was tall and had very long legs, so I fancied that I could have been a bikini model if it had not been for my arm. How telling: as an adolescent, my dream job was to be a bikini model! For many adolescents it is not the actual job of being a model that appeals; it is the kudos, the knowledge that one's body has been declared special. Worthy of attention. 'If I looked that way, then they would love me . . .'

At school, I hid my scars not only with the sleeves of my jumper but also by seeming self-assured. I knew that if I appeared vulnerable, I would be targeted. So I spent my free time joining in with my peers rating one another. I went to an all-girls school and at lunchtime it was as if the magazines we read, which told us what clothes were in and whether a celebrity was hot or not, had sprung to life. We may not have been able to control many elements of our lives, but we could definitely control one another through ridicule. The ratings we gave one another might not have been held up like scores in a talent show, but they were branded on our psyches.

The rules in girls' rating games, then and now, are not difficult to follow. Be considered hot by your peers, in particular by boys, and you score points. Getting a highly desired boyfriend means an instant advance to the top of the club. I was lucky enough to land the school 'spunk' from the boys' school next door and was elevated from classroom 'brainiac' to the girl everyone wanted to know, almost overnight. He dumped me a year later for a girl considered hotter. At just 14, she was a fashion model appearing in women's magazines and parading in labels sold only to rich 30-somethings.

My dream run at the top of the charts was over. I had all my deepest fears confirmed. The prettiest girl did win. In my mind, the breakup was all about me not being beautiful enough. It seemed all the more tragic because I had elevated him to godlike status for loving me despite my scars.

Looking back, I see how ridiculous this all was. I was funny, bright, passionately in love with him. He was not doing me any favours by being with me! It seems strange to me now that at no stage did I stop and think that perhaps my relationship with this boy had broken down for reasons other than my appearance. Possibly it had been the pressure of us getting too serious too soon (the reason my boyfriend gave me at the time), or maybe we were just growing apart. He may have just been a jerk. And the truth is, while the new girl certainly was beautiful, she may have been so much more than just her looks, too.

It was only in my adult years, as a teacher, that I finally explored ways in which I might come to terms with my burns. If I could not accept myself, how could I possibly ask my students to accept themselves?

I searched once again for soothing words, and found them in the writing of women such as Naomi Wolf, who wrote in *The Beauty Myth*: 'We don't need to change our bodies, we need to change the rules.' In women such as Sophia Loren: 'Nothing makes a woman more beautiful than the belief that she is beautiful.' And in the words of the young women I now taught: 'I love how you wear your scars, Miss, you don't let them wear you.' Words healed me. And my self-talk once more became focused on my strengths rather than my perceived weaknesses. I *was* okay. It *would be* all right.

And everything was okay. And it was more than just all right. Life without self-doubt was magnificent. I loved and I was loved. As a confident 20-something, I shone. I have a picture of me taken back then, when I went to the Amazon, in South America, for my honeymoon. It captures the authentic me. I look strong, fit. I am wearing a singlet top and grinning from ear to ear. I had been trekking in the jungle with my new husband and we had stumbled upon a village. When the local children saw my burn scars they ran and hid from me. Our guide explained that they feared I would die soon as they were not used to seeing large scars. In the Amazon, as there is no running water or electricity, if you get a major injury you will most likely die from infection. I assured our guide that he should tell the children I was fine. And one by one, they came across and touched my arm, played with my hair, and started telling me in the local language that I was a strong, brave girl. A warrior girl.

Yes. I am an Amazon warrior. I am more than my body. It is such a small part of the entire Dannielle Miller story that it has again been relegated to a co-starring role. I have managed to move from hating my body to not just accepting it but loving it, scars and all. I don't think it is perfect, but I am okay with that. This is me.

When I choose to indulge in the trappings of conventional beauty – heels and hair dye – I do so knowing that these things may be fun, and they may make me feel pampered or be just what my outfit calls for on a special occasion, but they do not make me worth more or ensure I will be loved. I feel equally as valuable when I'm at home wearing my ugg boots and track pants, with my hair pulled back in an unbrushed mop. And though I may get occasionally frustrated with my tummy, I cannot bring myself to hate it for a moment. It is part of me. My body is like a dear friend: not perfect, yet lovable and comforting, quirks and all. Despite the advertising rhetoric, diets, surgery and cosmetics do not have some mystical power that will bring us eternal happiness. I know this.

How liberating! And, unfortunately, how rare. Many girls will not grow to be women who love their bodies. They will believe that if they just had the right-shaped breasts, or a flatter tummy, or a smaller nose, their life would be complete. They will bear scars of their own for many years – it's just that their scars may not be quite as obvious as mine.

At war with the body

Many girls are enslaved to their bodies. Their supposed imperfections – be they scars, weight or bust size – take on monstrous proportions. This deprives them of finding that Amazon power within. Statistics tell the story bluntly: 94 per cent of teenage girls wish, some of the time, that they were more beautiful. A quarter of teenage girls want to change everything physically about themselves.

The problem with statistics is that it is easy for us to be emotionally detached and for the numbers to become somewhat meaningless. But each number is a real girl. A girl who wakes up hungry and chooses to stay that way all day. A girl who is deeply sad. A girl who feels that she is unloved and unlovable. A girl who limps through her days hiding, through actual physical withdrawal or by assuming an 'I am sooo fine' façade, or by ridiculing others to deflect attention away from herself. Living with a sense of inadequacy hurts; occasionally this girl will take the ache from within her own chest and throw it at other girls, allowing herself just that little bit of breathing space. This teen girl might tease and belittle others, because it deflects attention away from her own perceived flaws.

I have cried for, and with, many of the girls I have worked with, as they shared with me the pain of being at war with their own bodies.

> I have struggled since I was six with weight and body image . . . I haven't eaten for a week in an attempt to be beautiful.
>
> Katia, 15

> My whole life, I have been called just 'that fat kid'.
>
> Lucy, 16

> I think I am not as pretty as other girls. I hate the way I look, as it means I can't make friends.
>
> Samantha, 12

> I don't like to look in mirrors or get my photo taken, 'cause I am not beautiful. None of the girls I see in magazines look like me, because my skin is really dark. I wish I could make it whiter.
>
> Stephanie, 13

Often, I do not cry out of sadness. My workshops are

incredibly joyful. I cry tears of joy and gratitude, too. I try to help heal and soothe and show girls that there is another way. Girls *can* silence their inner critic and begin a new conversation within, a conversation that affirms rather than destroys.

For this to happen, girls need new, positive messages, delivered with authenticity and passion. Girls need to see women who realise that they are so much more than just their bodies.

Making peace with the body

The first step towards supporting your daughter to rewrite her internal dialogue about her body is to listen to your own internal dialogue. If you are not yet at peace with yourself about your body, then your advice will not seem authentic and will not have credibility. Teenagers have amazing in-built lie detectors!

If you are still at war with your own body, you are far from alone. Many women are sucked into the same body-hating vortex. We tell our daughters they are beautiful the way they are, while we angst over our weight and wrinkles.

We have to make this right. We have to move beyond this. If you already have, well done. If you are still dealing with some body issues of your own, then firstly, let's attempt to shift things. In my workshops, I ask the girls to look at the source of their feelings of inadequacy about their bodies. This is an equally relevant and important starting point for us as women, too. We may have our own individual reasons for feeling uncomfortable with our appearance, such as an experience we had in the past; and body image is also profoundly shaped by social, political, racial, age and gender factors.

But there is something we all share: just like girls, we are at war with our bodies because there is a war being *waged on* our bodies. On an unprecedented scale, we are surrounded by words and images dictating what beauty is. The television shows we watch, the websites we browse, the music and radio stations we listen to, the newspapers and magazines we read – all of them bombard us with messages about what makes a woman beautiful, desirable and worthy. Almost none of these messages offer a healing or empowering idea of feminine beauty.

Advertising is perhaps the most noxious and inescapable culprit. The average person sees around 75 advertisements every day. We see them on television, in newspapers and magazines, on the sides of buses, on our streets, when we are surfing the net and even on the backs of toilet doors. One in every 11 commercials has a *direct* message about beauty, while countless others carry *indirect* messages about what makes a woman beautiful. An overwhelming number of times each day, we are told what we should look like.

And the definition of beauty presented to us has become increasingly narrow. It is now one colour, one shape, one size. The standards have become increasingly impossible to obtain.

I have to remind myself that I am a good person and so much more than just my looks; I have a great career, a gorgeous family . . . Having my own teen daughters helps because it forces me to re-evaluate what makes me really beautiful, for if I dwell on the superficial, then surely they will, too. I think for many women, making ourselves feel bad is a learned behaviour. It makes sense, then, that making ourselves feel good, and whole, needs to be learned, too.

Lynne, mother of a 15- and a 17-year-old girl

Starving for attention

Most fashion models today have the ultra-thin waif-like look epitomised by Kate Moss. During the last three decades, fashion and advertising models have grown steadily thinner, yet the average weight of women under 30 years of age has actually risen.

Various shapes and sizes have been considered ideal throughout history. In the seventeenth century, the time that Rubens was painting his masterpieces, fuller-figured women were highly desirable as their curves were an indication of wealth. Only poor working women were thin, so thinness was associated with being lower class. In the 1950s – not all that long ago, really – the voluptuous actress Marilyn Monroe was considered the ultimate sex goddess. She dated presidents, sports stars and gangsters, was adored and imitated (although even she was not happy and lived with constant, almost debilitating self-doubt), but today would probably be told by movie executives to lose weight.

Fast forward and what do Hollywood celebrities look like now? On the oh-so-cool website of stylist to the stars Patricia Field, of *Sex and the City* fame, I found this must-have item for budding fashionistas: the Trash and Luxury Celebrity Diet shirt: 'Another amazing celeb inspired tee.

The celebrity diet, and our diet. Complete with a balanced cigarette, and some pills . . . any pills.' No doubt that's meant to be tongue-in-cheek – but it actually does a good job of evoking the current celebrity stick-thin female ideal.

Hollywood stars are quite literally banking on their looks, but they aren't the only ones who are obsessed with the elusive body beautiful. Many of us have dieting down to an art form too, substituting cigarettes, pills and faddish concoctions for real food. Some purge through vomiting or laxatives, or have surgery. Our relationship with food, which surely should be so simple, seems to have become incredibly complex. Health experts warn that we are simultaneously in the midst of an obesity epidemic; Australian Bureau of Statistics figures show that up to 54 per cent of the adult population may be over-weight. Large numbers of women and girls routinely go on diets: as many as 50 per cent of teenage girls say they have been on a diet. Tragically, all this dieting and suffering does not even work. Within two years, 95 per cent of people who go on weight-loss diets, including commercial diets, regain all the weight they lost, plus more. No wonder the weight-loss industry is worth billions of dollars each year: once its slave, we are forever in its service.

Then there is the even darker side of weight loss: the eating disorders anorexia and bulimia. Many of us have self-doubt and days when we wish we were more attractive. For some, however, mental illness and a serious body–mind disconnect may arise in adolescence. Although people of all ages and both sexes are affected by eating disorders, they are most common in adolescent girls and young women. Some recent studies have shown the number of adolesecent girls who fit the diagnostic criteria for eating disorders may be as high as 20 per cent – that's one in five – among students. At least one in five teen girls resort to extreme dieting measures, such as laxatives. A Victorian study of adolescents aged 12 to 17 years classified 38 per cent of girls and 12 per cent of boys as intermediate to extreme dieters, that is, at risk of an eating disorder. A Sydney study of adolescents aged 11 to 15 reported that 16 per cent of the girls and 7 per cent of the boys had already employed at least one potentially dangerous method of weight reduction, including starvation, vomiting and laxative abuse.

It has become accepted that we should all be dissatisfied with our bodies and should all be striving to become thinner, more toned, a more 'perfect' shape. As Courtney Martin says in her book *Perfect Girls, Starving Daughters*, 'We can be well educated, creative, capable, experienced, and still not have the capacity to figure out how to free ourselves from guilt over every little thing we put in our mouths.'

The new normality of hating one's body is evident everywhere. It certainly rates well on TV. The Australian version of the ultimate diet show, *The Biggest Loser*, launched its 2008 season with advertisements that showed sad, lonely-looking people – depicted in shades of grey – who wanted far more than just a healthy body. The ad that really struck me featured the contestant Nicola. 'I just want to be like every other girl,' she declared. Nicola did lose weight, dramatically. Yes, after much blood, sweat, tears and a good dose of public humiliation, she got her 'reveal', a night when all the contestants paraded their new bodies to gasping audiences. I don't know whether she got the acceptance and love she so obviously craved, but the irony was that Nicola already was like every other girl: she saw her body as the enemy.

The Biggest Loser's theme song was Beck's 'Everyone's Gotta Learn Sometimes', which includes the lyric 'I need your lovin'.' Isn't that what we all really crave – love? It's just that some of us get lost and think we might find love in food and then get bewildered when society tells us we will find it only through our hunger. There is a known link between our emotions and what we eat, yet it seems to be largely ignored by all the hype that surrounds each diet fad or regime that seductively promises a new life through a new body.

Becoming skinny doesn't guarantee us happiness or love.

> There is a huge amount of pressure on girls to be thin.
>
> Anon., 15

> The hardest thing about being a teenage girl is living with the media telling us continuously how to look.
>
> Anon., 15

Diet is not the only seemingly straightforward part of life that has become fraught for women and girls. Exercise is another body battleground. It seems self-evident that we should all try to get regular exercise to stay fit and healthy, but so often advertising and the media focus on a less healthy motivation. Being a woman itself is portrayed as a competitive sport; exercising is not so much about being fit as about trying to perfect our appearance. This, we are told, will make us more desirable, give us an advantage over other women and make them envious.

Skins, a range of sportswear for women, offered some ultra-destructive messages with their 2008 campaign: 'Men will love you, women will hate you. Lucky you're not a lesbian. Skins delivers immediate results for the woman who wants to look and feel like a complete bitch.' Or how about: 'Get a body to die for. And watch women queue up to help with your funeral arrangements. Skins are perfect for the woman who loves the feel of claws sticking into her back.'

The emphasis on playing sport or exercising merely as a means of obtaining the perfect body is ugly enough, but pitting woman against woman? Grotesque.

Also ugly was the Brooks Sports ad that promoted the company's support of breast cancer treatment. This is a great cause, but their promotion featured two female runners with their breasts bouncing and the caption 'Nice pair!'

The sportswear may not be revealing, but the advertising campaigns certainly are: exercise just to look hot, hot, hot. These ads feed the very real risk of girls exercising excessively as a means of controlling weight. Research clearly shows excessive exercise and eating disorders go hand in hand.

These ads also alienate girls and women who may not be comfortable with ruthless competition, nor with being viewed as just a pair of tits in sneakers. It is not always easy to get girls active and messages such as these really don't help. Getting girls to have a healthy level of activity is so essential that in 2006 there was an Australian Senate Inquiry into female participation in sport. One of the inquiry's conclusions was that female sportswear might be a deterrent to participation. If their recent ad campaigns are anything to go by, it seems that sportswear manufacturers haven't entirely heeded the report, which called for sportswear that is flattering, comfortable and practical. If this is a cause of body anxiety for your daughter, try speaking to her school to see if it is possible to allow girls some input into designing their own sports uniforms. Perhaps options could be provided to allow more personal choice, such as looser designs.

Girls and women urgently need more positive messages about being fit and healthy and participating in sport, such as one Adidas women's campaign: 'Play a sport where the rewards are respect, self belief and inner strength. Play by your own rules. Play gym. Impossible is nothing.' Yes!

The camera always lies

So much of the idea of beauty that we are trying to live up to is not even real. The trend towards digitally manipulating away supposed imperfections – including those features that make us unique and interesting – affects virtually every image we see in advertisements and many of the images we see of celebrities. Once the photographer's job was to capture what was beautiful and individual about a model or star. Today, their photographs are altered until they fit a socially accepted standard of flawless beauty.

But it is not just the glossy magazines and advertisers that crop, colour, erase and enhance their images. Ordinary people want a bit of the action, too: there is a roaring trade in touching up photos for social networking sites such as facebook and MySpace. British chain Snappy Snaps made the news when it saw requests for its digital touch-up service rise by 550 per cent in just a three-month period. Cheekbones are elongated; freckles are banished; braces are even removed. How much longer until all the images we see of women will blur into the one homogenised, unobtainable version of beauty?

We play the 'compare and despair' game, comparing images of women who seem perfect, but are not real, to our bodies, which are real. And for some, despair turns to a desire to cut and paste – not on a computer screen, but in real life.

Plastic not so fantastic

Our differences, our imperfections and our physical scars make us unique. Yet the messages we receive through the media tell us that our differences set us apart for all the wrong reasons.

Celebrities are beginning to morph into one another. Many feature the same bee-stung lips, chiselled cheekbones, wide eyes and wrinkle-free brow, a look now so fashionable and commonplace that *New York* magazine coined a term for it. The 'New New Face' – a plumped-up 'baby' face made possible by the latest advancements in cosmetic surgery – is epitomised by such stars as Madonna, Demi Moore, Michelle Pfeiffer and Liz Hurley.

Women are no longer permitted to age and must remain forever taut, trim and vigilant against the ravages of time – although euphemistically we are told we will just be 'refreshed' and 'rejuvenated'. And can it really be so bad when it seems that just about everyone is doing it?

Reality television displays a distinct preference for young women who are in love with their fresh new breasts. Krystal Forscutt and her mother had matching breast enlargements before they entered the *Big Brother* house. In September 2008, men's magazine *Ralph* featured another *Big Brother* evictee, Bridgette, who was dressed in the mandatory provocative lingerie, proudly displaying her breast enhancements. Disturbingly, she was also surrounded by children's cuddly toys and had a baby's dummy in her hand. She complimented housemate Bianca's large breasts and said that if she was prime minister of Australia, she would 'probably give everyone free boob jobs. I think guys would appreciate the girls getting them.'

While it is easy to dismiss her words as the inane ranting of a wannabe, the fact remains that plastic surgery and other cosmetic procedures are being used by women in the mainstream as a means of seeking the attention and validation they crave. And it seems that it is no longer enough to have a facelift or a boob job, or to have some collagen injected in our lips. Vaginal 'rejuvenation' procedures are now popular, too. It seems everything female needs to be reshaped.

It is not that hard to understand why women might want faces and bodies that look more like the stars', but why the desire for a designer vagina? 'Now women shave,' said Dr Gary J. Alter, a plastic surgeon and urologist with offices in Beverly Hills and Manhattan, who has come up with his own 'labia contouring' technique. 'Now they see porn. Now they're more aware of appearance.'

It is no longer just the rich and famous who have become fans of the scalpel. American plastic surgeon Dr Michael Salzhauer has even published a picture book for children that attempts to explain their mothers' impending surgery, *My Beautiful Mommy*. The mother in this story explains to her daughter why she needs surgery: 'You see, as I got older, my body stretched and I couldn't fit into my clothes any more. Dr Michael is going to help fix that and make me feel better.'

But will she really *feel* better? Does changing our bodies really guarantee a change of heart? It is a myth that plastic surgery improves self-esteem. In fact, some studies have shown high rates of depression and even suicidal thoughts in women after they have breast enhancements.

We are sending damaging messages to our young girls when we chop to change. Worse still, Botox is actually being pitched to young women as a 'preventive' against wrinkles. In an online game aimed at teenage girls, Miss Bimbo, players earn credits towards diet pills and cosmetic surgery.

Just harmless fun? No. This is insane.

It is important to realise we have the power to resist and change the harmful stereotypes presented to women as the ideals for which we must strive.

We have the power to create our own new body-loving reality.

We have an obligation – to ourselves and to our daughters – to end the madness.

Action plan

Be a good role model.

Your daughter watches, listens and learns through you how to treat her own body. Don't underestimate the power you have to influence her, for better or worse. Media expert Professor Catharine Lumby from the University of New South Wales undertook a three-year study on young girls and their media consumption. She says of her research: 'There's no question that girls were very aware of pressures on them about appearance but they felt this didn't just come from the media, it also came from things like behaviour modelled by their mothers.' Stop weighing yourself; stop compulsively dieting; stop talking about how unhappy you are with your appearance. Easier said than done, I know, but professional help is available, if you need it.

Tell your daughter you love her for who she is, not how she looks. When I tell my daughter she is beautiful, I make sure I praise at least two qualities in her that I also admire, e.g. 'You are beautiful *and* smart, funny, kind-hearted, passionate, strong, brave, intelligent . . .' Australia's sex discrimination commissioner and the commissioner responsible for age discrimination, Elizabeth Broderick, told me she has long chats about body image with her daughter, who she believes is far more concerned with body image than she was as a girl. Elizabeth told me, 'I asked her once "Who loves Lucy the best?" She answered, "Mummy, Daddy." I corrected her: "No, Lucy must love Lucy the best." I believe she will learn this partly through the way we demonstrate our love for her.'

Choose your words carefully when you talk about your daughter's appearance. Girls can be hypersensitive about references to their body and are excellent at picking up the subtle messages that may not even be expressed openly. Snide remarks about weight or appearance will be absorbed into the soul.

Get Dad on side, too. The way a father figure treats and talks about the women in the family and women in general has a powerful effect, as the first experience your daughter has with the male gaze is his. The comedian Dawn French provides a particularly moving example of how influential fathers can be in her sublime book *Dear Fatty*. Dawn recalls when her father told her she was 'an uncommon beauty, a dazzling, exquisite, splendid young woman'. She reflects: 'My dad gave me armour that night and I have worn it ever since. I could never quite buy the bit about being the best, but I *do* believe I am worth something. My self-esteem, still surprisingly intact after quite a few attacks, is still my strong centre, my metal, and I owe that to him.'

Encourage healthy diet and exercise rather than pushing your daughter to lose weight. One of the most practical things girls can do to promote a healthy body image is become involved in sports. Research both here and in the United States has found that women who participate in sports and physical activity have a more positive body image than those who don't. Participation in sports brings approval from peers, family and friends, and helps women feel that they are capable and competent. These positive feelings produce a positive body image.

Empathise.
It's unrealistic and unfair to simply dismiss your daughter's concern with appearances. To us adults, it may seem frivolous or unimportant, but in teen-girl world, fitting in and being seen to belong is considered vital. Appearance is one tangible means adolescents use to compare and contrast one another. Rather than trivialising her concerns, you can help her gain perspective. Encourage her to see other attractive qualities in the girls around her and in herself. Be kind to her and encourage her to be kind to others.

Watch for early warning signs of a serious body-image crisis. Early warning signs of an eating disorder may include any or a combination of the following: dramatic weight loss, constant dieting, excessive exercising, social withdrawal, a fixation with food, a change in appetite (either refusing to eat or bingeing) and insomnia. Seek professional help, even if she tells you there is nothing to be alarmed about; girls who are suffering from eating disorders are often in denial.

A number of teen girls also self-harm. In the practice known as 'cutting', girls use sharp objects to make incisions on their bodies, especially their arms or upper legs. Girls who self-harm may also burn or hit themselves. Warning signs include scars or frequent unexplained injuries. This behaviour is often a response to stress and anxiety about body image, academic expectations, destructive relationships or any of the other issues that girls might face. It should be brought to the attention of a health professional.

You can find more about eating disorders and self-harm in Chapter 7, 'Rage and Despair: Girls in Crisis'.

Help your daughter navigate the media.
Although I do not think the media is solely responsible for the objectification of women, I do think it plays a key role. Pay attention to what your daughter reads, watches and listens to. Young people need to become critical viewers of popular culture and should be given the tools to deconstruct media messages. Encourage your daughter to become an active viewer and reader, rather than passively absorbing media messages. Pose questions such as 'Why do you think all the actresses on this show are the same body shape and size?', 'How do you feel about your body after reading that magazine?' or 'Do you think it will be easy for this contestant to maintain that body shape after they leave the program?'

There are some excellent websites, magazines and books listed in Appendix 4, Resources, that are well worth accessing.

Start a Detox Diary together.
Despite what the media tells us, our bodies are not toxic. We do not constantly need to detox to purge and rid ourselves of poisons. Yet our minds may be in need of a cleanse. A Detox Diary is a record of healing and of your journey from hating to loving your own body. The following are just some of the things that can be included:
- images of women who inspire you
- notes and letters from friends that make you feel good about yourself
- affirmations such as those included throughout this book
- quotes that motivate you
- photographs of you looking and feeling happy.

Encourage your daughter to start a Detox Diary and start one yourself. If you feel comfortable doing so, perhaps you might even like to share your diaries with each other. Your diaries should not focus on negative thoughts, fears and insecurities about your bodies. While writing such things down can prove cathartic, I believe there is also a real risk that it encourages you to obsess on the negatives, revisiting them over and over, and reopening old wounds.

Appreciate your body.
Women's bodies are amazing. I could not believe it when I first breastfed: how did my breasts know how to create milk? My body instinctively held the secret to nourishing life. Instead of critiquing yourself, celebrate the parts of your body you are pleased with. Focus on the positive aspects and give them a new emphasis.

See yourself as a whole person.
You are more than just your breasts, your butt, your thighs – just as I am so much more than my arm. When we see ourselves and other women – including our daughters – as just our bodies, we forget that we are actually *somebodies*.

I was once shocked by a conversation I had with a teacher after I had just spent an amazing day with her students, who had been captivated and loved every minute of our workshop. This teacher had sat talking (loudly) to other members of staff the whole time. I thought she had not listened to a word.

I was only partially correct. That evening, as I was about to address the girls' parents, she said to me, 'I heard parts of your opening talk to the girls this morning. You were burnt? Doesn't matter. At least your face is still pretty.' What could I say to this? She had missed the point entirely: my real beauty has very little to do with any physical part of me. Fortunately, it seemed her students had heard my message. Each of these little girls had lined up to kiss and hug me at the end of the day; and when they told me I was beautiful, I knew they had seen all of me.

See all of yourself and all of your daughter.

Highlight other healthy role models.
In a world where trashy celebrities adorn most magazines, it can be challenging to find good female role models, but it is an important quest. My daughter and I have both been drawn to a fictional female role model, Wonder Woman. And we do not love her just for her star-spangled ensemble. Wonder Woman is one very smart sister. When all the other superheroes lined up for their super powers, they asked for things such as x-ray vision, the ability to sling webs or super-human speed. Wonder Woman, an Amazon, asked for the 'lasso of truth'. Her gold rope surrounds the bad guys and forces them to speak words of truth to her. Words do have such power, the words we are surrounded by and those we use ourselves.

A great resource for role models is the American web-site The REAL Hot 100 – www.therealhot100.com – which profiles young women who are achieving and challenging themselves and their communities. It is helpful to remember, too, that not *all* celebrities are pole dancing and passing out in LA hotspots every night: the web site www.celebrityrole-model.com aims to highlight only good celebrity behaviour.

Actress Kate Winslet is one of the few Hollywood stars who tells it like it is. She once said in an interview:

I don't want the next generation, your daughters and mine, growing up thinking that you have to be thin to look beautiful in certain clothes. It's terrifying right now. It's out of control. It's beyond out of control . . . I feel an enormous responsibility to stay normal and true to myself and not conform and all those things. You know? To be healthy. And normal. And to like to eat cake.

May the truth set us free from the myth of the ideal woman.
We all deserve to eat cake.

Affirmations

I am more than my body;
I am my heart, soul and mind.
My body is strong, unique and beautiful.

3

Beyond Generation Bratz

❧

Most dolls for little girls nowadays are designed to represent teenage girls or women. One exception is Mattel's My Scene, Growing Up Glam™ doll, which depicts a tween, a girl aged 8–12 years. She is dressed in lacy stockings, short skirt, diamanté belt and midriff top. Her accessories? A teddy bear and schoolbooks.

Twist the screw on her back – oh, how symbolic! – and her abdomen lengthens. It's gruesome to watch. She looks as though she is being lenghtens by a medieval torture device. And hey presto, now she's a 'curvy, cool teen'. But wait, you say, all that has really changed is that her stomach has stretched to make her taller.

How telling. It seems that in Mattel land there is no difference between an 8-year-old girl and an 18-year-old one. Nor should the clothes they wear differ. The only things that change once she has stretched before our very eyes into a 'curvy, cool teen' are her accessories. She trades in her schoolbooks and teddy bear for a full make-up kit, complete with false eyelashes – 'Whoa, her make-up changes!' – and some glossy fashion magazines. Flat shoes are out; it's all about stilettos now. Out, too, with the cute hair clips and in with the designer sunnies.

Where do I begin in explaining why I think this type of doll is so toxic for our daughters?

'Curvy.' This is not a word we used to associate with little girls or even with girls in their early teens. Yet look around. We now live in a culture that tells our young girls that being hot, thin, sexy – and useless – is *way* cool.

For the good of our girls, women and for our society generally, it is time to take stock. Teen girls are increasingly being portrayed in a highly sexualised way and even their younger sisters are being encouraged to be sexy. Are we really all okay with that?

Too sexy, too soon

Many people – including leading experts in education, health and psychology – have serious concerns that the current cultural climate imposes pressure on girls to be too sexy, too soon.

We aren't talking about the healthy development of

sexuality here. It is perfectly normal for children as they grow and develop to explore their sexuality; and there is nothing wrong with providing children with age-appropriate information and education about sex.

What *is* wrong is when a child has sexuality inappropriately imposed on them. This is known by experts as 'sexualisation'. When a child displays a more adult sexuality, 'it is often imposed upon them rather than chosen by them', according to the American Psychological Association (APA). In their definition of 'sexualisation', the APA also includes when a person's value comes only from their sexual appeal; their sexiness is judged according to a narrow ideal of physical attractiveness; or they are sexually objectified, that is, seen simply as an object for others' sexual use.

These elements can all be seen, to varying degrees, in the influences young girls are growing up with. A large body of research shows that exposure to sexualised imagery is linked to children experiencing increased anxiety, depression, low self-esteem, body-image problems, eating disorders, and self-harm. The APA set up a taskforce on the sexualisation of girls; it reported that sexualisation has a negative effect on girls' 'cognitive functioning, physical and mental health, sexuality and beliefs'. The Australian Psychological Society is so concerned about this issue that it has released guidelines for parents regarding the early sexualisation of children.

In the toy store
The vile Growing Up Glam tween-to-teen doll is certainly not exceptional in promoting a sexy look. Even good old Barbie,

who has previously been portrayed as a teacher, astronaut and even as a US presidential candidate, is now doused in glitter, wears micro-miniskirts and has been given the obligatory party-girl accessories. Mattel's Bling Bling Bikini doll comes with bikini, stilettos, thick make-up, optional bling bling spa and what looks to me like a pina colada cocktail as an accessory.

Bratz dolls are still in the top ten bestseller list at Christmas. Sportz Bratz carries the slogan 'It is not how you play, but about how hot you look when you win.' Even baby dolls are given the sexed-up treatment. The Baby Bratz range features toddlers wearing G-string-style lingerie, fish-nets, leather micro-minis and chain belts. These baby dolls have moved way beyond prams: they come complete with Harley-Davidson-style motorbikes.

Does it really matter? Yes. It really does. Childhood plus the adult world of fish-nets, booze, and grown-up confidence and attitude makes a dangerous combination.

It would be too simplistic to argue that it is dolls alone that are damaging our daughters, yet when we buy these toys for our girls we are buying into an insidious trend to steal the innocence of childhood. Girls mature physically and emotionally more rapidly than boys and also tend to be more quickly immersed in popular culture; therefore, their childhood is already particularly brief. Why are we allowing their little-girl time to be even more rapidly eroded?

And if it is okay to buy a lingerie-clad Baby Bratz reclining on a revolving bed under a disco light, just what is off limits for our girls?

At the magazine stand

The fact is that currently nothing seems to be off limits. Even media that purport to care about and empower girls have sold them out by sexing them up. *Girlpower* is an Australian magazine aimed at girls aged from 7 to 12. When I was flipping through an issue, I found images that were anything but empowering. They included a poster of Ashlee Simpson for little girls to put on their bedroom walls. It showed the singing star wearing a man's suit with no top underneath and not even a bra. She was pulling the waistband of her trousers down to show more of her crotch and though she didn't show her nipple, her left breast was mostly exposed. Ashlee's real source of power – her voice – was negated: her mouth was shut. Her eyes were downcast and much of her face was veiled by her long blonde hair. It was all about her body.

The same issue also included a 'Hotness Scale' that encouraged small girls to have a crush on Nick Lachey. At 35, the singer and former husband of pop diva Jessica Simpson is older than many of their fathers. Also singled out was 23-year-old Chace Crawford, a star of *Gossip Girl*. That's an M-rated TV show and therefore one they shouldn't even be watching yet. Surely Jessica Simpson's ex and an actor who plays a bad-boy pothead who needs to go to rehab are not ideal boyfriends for little girls. Magazines that encourage primary-school-age girls to have crushes on men are playing a dangerous game with their minds. We do our utmost to protect our children. To cultivate mature men as romantic ideals for little girls seems at odds with those efforts.

It is actually impossible for parents to critique many of

the magazines aimed at primary-school-aged girls before purchasing them, as they are sealed in plastic to protect all the giveaways they entice readers with. It is ironic that the men's magazines also displayed at children's eye height in supermarkets are not sealed in plastic and can be scrutinised by curious eyes. Magazines such as *FMH*, *Ralph* and *Zoo*, showing scantily clad bikini babes on the front, are purchased at all our major supermarkets while buying the milk and bread. I don't want my children viewing soft porn while I am grabbing cordial off the shelf.

Elements of the soft-porn men's magazine world meet the teen-girl world head-on by the time high school girls start consuming magazines such as *Girlfriend* and *Dolly*. These magazines also find an audience in younger girls, often featuring letters from readers that are 11, 12 or 13 years old. And why wouldn't parents purchase these publications for their curious daughters? *Girlfriend* purports to be 'a girl's best friend' and to focus on empowering girls. Yet in 2007 it ran a giveaway of Playboy t-shirts. Readers were told:

> Playboy is a collection of clothing and swimwear for the trend savvy fashionable girl. Cute and innocent, cool and tough, all at the same time. Playboy is one brand you should include in your wardrobe.

Playboy has long been a leading brand in the pornography industry, but more recently it has been insidiously creeping into the mainstream. Porn-inspired pencil case anyone? I recently worked with Year 5 girls at a school and found that already, by the age of ten, around a quarter of them claimed they read *Girlfriend*. One girl also proudly told me that she already had a Playboy t-shirt, too. 'It's really cute,' she said. 'It is striped with the bunny on the left corner.' (The teachers later told me that this little girl's naivety paled in comparison to that of another girl who, at a school camp, wore a t-shirt with the slogan 'Wrap your lips around this' emblazoned across the front. The girl, who happened to be a particularly reserved child, had no idea how inappropriate this was. Apparently, nor did her parents.)

There is inherent hypocrisy in a teen magazine claiming to empower girls while promoting a brand related to the porn industry. Not to mention that the publishers who produce *Girlfriend* also briefly published *Explode*, a magazine for teen boys that boasts 'all the eye candy you can handle'. Sounds like blatant objectification of girls' bodies to me.

The current editor of *Girlfriend* sits on the government's National Body Image advisory group, and while recent issues of the magazine have featured some useful articles, some of the ads are still giving conflicting toxic messages.

In the advertising sections at the back of *Girlfriend* and *Dolly*, ads for mobile phone ringtones and wallpaper downloads predominate. Many of the messages are highly sexual and offer an unhealthy perspective on girls and their emerging sexuality: 'Save a virgin, do me instead.' 'Fancy a quickie anyone?' 'Sex – when it's good, it's really good, when it's bad, it's still pretty good.'

I appreciate that editor's may not be able to revolutionise their magazines overnight, and I suspect that in our current economic climate they may be even less selective about the advertising they accept, but if they are serious about their commitment to young women they simply must be more vigilant.

Some of the information on sex contained in these magazines is very informative and sensible; and magazines can and do play an important role in educating girls about their budding sexuality. Yet I fear that in some cases they risk leading their readers to think that if they are not yet sexually active, they are missing out. In the results of a sex survey in *Dolly*, 21 per cent of readers were quoted as claiming to have lost their virginity at between 10 and 13 years of age. Do we think it is acceptable that a fifth of *Dolly*'s readers say they lost their virginity at between 10 and 13 years of age? The legal age of consent is 16. Either a lot of young girls are engaging in sexual activities before they are perhaps psychologically or emotionally mature enough to do so – or a lot of young girls exaggerate, as they think sexiness equates to coolness. Both possibilities are alarming. Just over half of readers were cited as saying they had given oral sex to a boy. For teen girls, fitting in and being accepted by their peers is all-important. There is a very real risk that young girls who read these magazines will think that to fit in and be part of the teen-girl community, they have to be sexually experienced. No one likes to feel left out.

On the internet

The sad reality is that for many children, pornography will be their first experience with sex; and fellatio tends to feature prominently in pornography. Porn is nothing new but it has never been more accessible than it is today, thanks to the internet and mobile phones. In the 2009 UK television series *The Sex Education Show*, three out of ten high school students interviewed said they learnt about sex predominantly through viewing pornography on the internet and mobiles or in magazines. In episode one, teens of both sexes were unimpressed when they were shown images of real breasts, which don't sit up like silicone-enhanced ones, and gasped in what seemed to be shock or disgust at images of women with pubic hair. Presenter Anna Richardson surmised: 'What's sad is they are putting pressure on themselves and each other, convinced by the sexual imagery they see that porn-star plastic is perfection.' Teenage girls in schools tell me that they are expected to act and look like the images their peers see on the thousands of sex sites they view online. This helps explain the fact that so many teenage girls now get Brazilian waxes. They see the look modelled by the women on porn sites and believe exposing their genitals in this way will make them hotter.

The web site girl.com.au claims to be empowering girls worldwide – but in 2008, I saw on their site another sad example of how the word 'empowering' has become so misused in our society. Their home page at the time featured Play School, Fisher-Price, Barbie and Bratz, so their target audience would seem to have included very young girls. Yet by clicking through to another page on girl.com.au, a reader would find a feature devoted to Brazilian waxing. Its advice for the little girls who logged on to be 'empowered' was:

Brazilian waxing involves spreading hot wax on your buttocks and vagina area. A cloth is patted over the wax, then pulled off. Don't be alarmed if the waxer throws your legs over your shoulder, or asks you to moon them, this is normal and ensures there are no stray hairs. A tweezer is used for the more delicate areas (red bits). So why does it appeal? Nobody really likes hair in their private regions and it has a childlike appeal. Men love it, and are eternally curious about it.

After I exposed this incredibly dangerous advice on my blog – since when should vaginas have a 'childlike appeal'? – the company took out the line about children's genitals being appealing. However, the page on Brazilian waxing, along with features on such topics as how to be a 'witch in the bedroom', remained.

It is little wonder that Brazilian waxing has become standard when girls have become accustomed to images of porn. Teachers tell me girls have become so desensitised that when the boys send them pornographic pictures via mobile phone with messages like 'You should make your pussy look like this one,' the girls simply laugh and forward the images on to other girls. In fact, 'sexting – the practice of forwarding an image of your own genitals to a friend – has become alarmingly common in our playgrounds. Teens say they do this as it makes them feel 'liberated'.

It's funny. I have images on my phone of most of my friends naked. It's like a club, I guess. If you trust people you'll send them a shot.

Anon., 14

It would be too easy to blame the victims. How many times have you heard a commentator say that girls nowadays dress too grown up and act too raunchy? The fact is that it is very difficult to resist pressure to conform, particularly for adolescent girls, because in their world belonging is everything. I am betting that when they receive inappropriate material, the girls laugh to mask their embarrassment. Teen girls must juggle their schoolwork, complex friendships, boys and their eternal quest to be beautiful and thin – all while maintaining a Paris Hilton–like worldliness. No wonder so many girls report feeling stressed, depressed and anxious.

I want to be very clear here: I am not advocating locking girls away in towers. It is vital that all children are informed about sex. Sex between consenting adults is natural and can be enormous fun.

But to me it seems damaging for girls who are just developing their own sexuality to be influenced largely by porn-inspired examples of sexuality. I am concerned not just because there are too many hyper-sexualised messages bombarding our girls, but because the ideal being presented to them of female sexuality is so narrow. Just as we are told that only a leggy size-8 model can be truly beautiful, we are now being told that only a busty, wet and wild blonde can be truly sexy. It's all big (fake) breasts, pouts, pole dancing and male-fantasy soft porn.

Women's (and men's) sexuality is, in reality, so much more diverse and complicated.

There is also a danger that girls may make the assumption that the women they see in porn are all truly enjoying it and are somehow empowered by the experience of being in the sex industry. In fact, research shows that many only participate because they feel they have no other option; they may be financially desperate, drugged or even physically coerced.

And often the type of pornography our young people are exposed to is not soft-core porn or even simple garden-variety sex between consenting adults. The internet delights in catering to all sorts of sexual tastes; many sites show images that are simply X-rated. This is not liberation. This is not about girls feeling good and exploring their bodies and the bodies of their partners if they choose to. This is a very narrow Hugh-Heffneresque vision of sexuality. The images of sex girls are exposed to online are largely devoid of relationship or meaning.

But it's not just the images they see online and the magazines they read that tell our girls it is all about pole dancing and pubic hair maintenance . . .

In music videos

Song lyrics have always been filled with sexual innuendo and pushed society's boundaries but there is a new in-your-face misogyny in mainstream music. An extreme example would be the rap lyrics used in a 2008 study titled 'Ambivalent Sexism and Misogynistic Rap Music: Does Exposure to Eminem Increase Sexism?', published in the *Journal of Applied Social Psychology*. The researchers, who were keen to see whether rap music in particular increased sexist attitudes in young people, introduced the sample group to these charming lines, amongst others, from Eminem's song 'Kill You': '(AH!) Slut, you think I won't choke no whore, 'til the vocal cords don't work in her throat no more?' Surprisingly, the study found little evidence that this type of language – language that uses derogatory synonyms for women like 'slut' and 'whore' to define them as mere tools for male sexual gratification – *created* beliefs that did not already exist.

Even if sexist attitudes do not increase through exposure to misogynistic music, surely such lyrics that describe attempting to kill a woman – to silence her permanently – normalise, and indeed glorify, violence against women. The researchers did concede that 'At worst, we could conclude that rap music might exacerbate pre-existing tendencies' yet they still concluded there was little reason to suggest these songs be censored. Why would we not want to curb a pre-existing tendency to want to harm a woman or refer to her in a demeaning way?

And, equally as importantly, what is the impact of being surrounded by misogynist lyrics on girls' and women's sense of self? How does hearing lyrics like these make girls and women feel about themselves and their bodies?

The American Academy of Pediatrics has stated that exposure to misogynistic music portraying sexual coercion and violence against women as normal may affect various aspects of young people's lives and may make it more difficult for them to know what is normal in a relationship.

There is also the fact that there seems to be a recording industry mandate that music videos have to sexually objectify women. Society's obsession with the current crop of sexy singing sirens was made very apparent when Scottish woman Susan Boyle rose to fame on the back of her performance on *Britain's Got Talent*. Prior to opening her mouth to sing, the judges and audience were seen laughing at her, almost embarrassed by her homely appearance. How dare she present herself as a singer! As someone worthy of our attention! The world was deeply shocked that she could actually sing. We have been seduced into equating attractiveness with talent.

Female stars apparently just can't sing if they're wearing more than lingerie and maybe a belt either. Male stars seem unable to perform unless surrounded by numerous pert breasts and gyrating rears. The camera angles used to film music videos are off-putting, too. More often than not, they seem to be shot with the camera looking up at the female performers' crotches; the girls I worked with at one school in New Zealand termed this technique 'crotch-cam'.

A British study found that watching video clips featuring skinny, semi-naked gyrating women – in other words, virtually all music clips – for just ten minutes was enough to reduce teenage girls' satisfaction with their body shape by 10 per cent. Yet look around: thanks to plasma screens in shopping centres, bowling alleys, you name it, these images are inescapable. This music is what we now give our children as the soundtrack to their youth. 'Hits for Kids, Volume 3' featured Hi-5, the cast of *Grease*, Guy Sebastian and . . . the Pussycat Dolls, a group of five women who have their origins in adult-only burlesque clubs. They gyrate, strut and pout their way through overtly sexy songs with lyrics that include: 'Don't cha wish your girlfriend was raw like me? Don't cha wish your girlfriend was fun like me?' These lyrics celebrate a particularly nasty brand of female competitiveness that is based on being the sexually overt.

Australian pop group The Veronicas (twins Jess and Lisa Origliasso) are also heavily marketed towards the tween demographic. They have a highly successful clothing range for girls aged 7 to 16, sold at Target stores, and are regular cover girls for tween-girl magazines. In interviews, the twins have acknowledged that fans as young as four go along to their concerts. Parents embraced their initial girl-power ethos and lyrics extolling the virtues of individuality: one of their first big hits, 'I'm a Revolution', celebrated their self-confidence.

So, what did their devoted tween fan base make of their 2008 single 'Take Me On The Floor'? The film clip is simply soft porn – shots of the now almost obligatory girl-on-girl kissing, lots of gyrating and close-ups of thighs being groped. The lyrics include an incredible amount of heavy breathing and the mantra 'I wanna kiss a girl, I wanna kiss a girl, I wanna kiss a boy, I wanna . . .' Meanwhile the dancers writhe uncontrollably as they all 'take each other' on the dance floor. (All this on Saturday morning TV, before I've even had my Vegemite on toast!)

My 10-year-old daughter had a Veronicas t-shirt.

After listening to their second album, I threw it in the bin.

Don't get me wrong, there have been amazing female singers and girl bands that have been all about power and strength – but today the groups most often said to epitomise girl power are really all about getting their gear off and pouting. The Pussycat Dolls, empowering? The Veronicas, a revolution? I don't see it. What I see is raunch culture being sold as empowerment.

One girl I worked with, Rose, told me: 'It really sucks being 13; I don't like it at all. There's just not much you can do and I feel older than this; I feel different, like maybe more like I am 15 . . . It is really important to me for some reason to have guys notice me . . . It makes me just feel special when boys look at me.' At a time when she is getting used to her developing sexuality and feeling more mature than her chronological age, it is easy to see how bands such as the Pussycat Dolls might have a potent influence on her. Rose went on to say, 'I do dance, hip hop. We have a concert at the end of the year and I love one costume as it is a corset. I look sexy in it. We are dancing to the Pussycat Dolls.'

Don't cha wish someone would stop this plot to steal childhood away? Don't cha wish someone would just use some common sense?

The great debate

Worries over the sexualisation of our children have become so intense that an Australian senate inquiry was called in 2008 to look into the issue. The inquiry was prompted by growing community concern and an Australia Institute report titled 'Corporate Paedophilia', a term used to describe advertising and marketing that sexualises children. The committee did confirm that children are certainly more sexualised, through the media they watch, the increased targeting of products to children and their greater exposure to information, particularly via the internet. Yet they also noted that 'it would be a mistake to equate these influences with actual harm.'

Why would it be a mistake to equate these influences with actual harm? Perhaps the committee reached this conclusion because of an absence of long-term research on the impact sexualisation has on children's physical and mental health. But does anyone think for one moment that any such research would come back showing that stealing childhood has actually been beneficial? We should not wait for more statistics to come in before we act. A large body of research has already alerted us to numerous potential dangers, including an increase in eating disorders, self-harm and risky sexual practices. Why can't we err on the side of caution when it comes to protecting children?

The senate committee made a range of recommendations to advertisers and the media to address the issue of child sexualisation, but those recommendations seemed to me to fall short of what is needed. Clive Hamilton, the former Director of the Australia Institute who oversaw the production of the report 'Corporate Paedophilia', summed up the inquiry's recommendations this way: '[They] amount to nothing more than a polite request that advertisers and broadcasters might perhaps, if it's not too much trouble, consider listening to community concerns a little more.'

The debate warmed up when *60 Minutes* gave it airtime. I was interviewed along with others who felt the inquiry didn't go far enough; a number of voices represented the other side of the argument, including the media expert Professor Catharine Lumby, from the University of New South Wales. Some of the critics of the inquiry were, she said, viewing children as 'uncovered meat'. Her concern was that children were being made to feel ashamed of their bodies. She noted how ridiculous it was that even nappy ads had been deemed inappropriate by a moral minority.

I agree with Catharine that it would be outrageous for anyone to suggest children's bodies are provocative. Banning nappy advertisements would be a silly and unnecessary knee-jerk reaction. But I believe that parents have real and valid concerns about hyper-sexual media and marketing. And I feel that most of us have fair and reasonable expectations. For instance, I don't have a problem with little girls wearing singlet tops – but I do have a problem with them wearing singlet tops featuring slogans such as 'Porn Star' or 'Tease'. And make no mistake, these are real examples of girls' clothing. Literally and metaphorically, these are the labels we are currently giving our tweens and young teens. Richard Eckersley in his book *Well and Good – Morality, Meaning and Happiness* voices the concerns of many:

> No sensible person would argue that there is a simple, direct relationship between media content and people's behaviour. But nor should any sensible person accept the proposition, implied by some cultural commentators, that what we see, hear and read in the media has no effect on us. Maybe children today are savvy, sophisticated consumers of media – as we are often told – but this does not mean that we can be complacent about media influences.

Take a stand

I believe we need government regulations that force advertisers and the media to act more responsibly; self-regulation obviously has not worked. Yet we cannot just absolve ourselves of responsibility and play victim to the vile marketers and product developers who want our girls to go straight from Play-Doh to pole dancing. After all, we are the ones buying this stuff for our children.

There are parents out there dressing their pre-teen daughters like life-size Bratz dolls. Some little girls are being put in padded lacy bras before a bra of any description is needed, or in shirts with slogans like 'Flirt'. Kids are wearing items from the Bratz clothing range, copied straight from the dolls' wardrobes. This marketing juggernaut has spun off into everything from real-life hyper-sexualised clothing to stationery and make-up. The latter includes gaudy eye shadows and fake leopard-print-tipped fingernails for girls five years and over, marketed as 'everyday glam'.

How can we as parents possibly look surprised when our girls at 13 want to dress in clothes like the ones we have been giving them to dress their dolls in for years? If we passively buy into the sexualisation of children – let alone if we actively encourage it with the clothes and toys we buy them – how can we possibly condemn girls who 'go wild' and pose provocatively on their MySpace pages in lingerie?

Like many little girls, my daughter used to do dancing – until one year at the annual Christmas concert I began feeling sick as I watched all the pint-size dancers dressed up and made up, like JonBenét Ramsey-style mini beauty queens. I had chosen Teyah's dance school as the teacher did not pressure the girls to be super-thin. Yet still, there was no escaping the obligatory hip wiggles and come-hither dance moves . . . from tiny tots. 'Aren't they cute?' many parents exclaimed. *Have we all gone insane?* I thought.

The clincher for me came after a routine based on the Austin Powers movies. A teenage girl in a long blonde wig and tiny shorts and midriff top did a super-sexy solo while the primary-school-aged mini Austin Powers boy dancers drooled on. Afterwards, the MC made a joke about the act waking up all the dads. Actually, all the dads near me looked deeply embarrassed through the routine: where to look? What to say? I wondered about the other little girls, such as my daughter who was only seven at the time, who sat watching in the wings, admiring the older girl during her routine. What messages did they take home that day about what it takes to get noticed?

Despite widespread community outrage, I really can't see advertisers and broadcasters backing off our children and ceasing to sexualise them. Sex sells – yes, even to tweens. So we must simply be more vigilant. Amanda Gordon, President of the Australian Psychological Society, offers this sage advice: 'I tell parents, "Don't buy sexy clothes for your children." There's nothing smart about having a four-year-old in a little bra. It's time for adults to take a stand, for parents to take a stand and say "This is what we want for our children" instead of children saying "This is what I want for me. . ." If the message is that you should be sexy and grown up, instead of being a kid, then kids aren't practising and learning how to be whole human beings . . . They are instead only imitating adult behaviour, without understanding it, and that's very dangerous for their development.'

The good news is that as parents we can have a positive influence over our girls' developing sexual identity. Recent British research indicates that parents can 'model' or reinforce particular responses to sexual material, and hence particular sexual identities for their children. We can and must create an ongoing dialogue with our daughters about the sexual messages, information and values they are exposed to in the media, in the playground and in our homes. We can and must be powerful voices of difference. And we must set boundaries.

I think before we can begin doing this, we need to establish a positive and non-judgemental attitude to our daughter's emerging sexuality, because in my experience, a negative or stigmatising attitude towards girls' sexual development may cause harm, particularly when it comes from parents, teachers or other trusted figures.

It can be confronting for us to accept that our children will grow up and become sexual beings. In general, our girls are physically growing up quicker. The age of puberty has consistently dropped in the West, from 17 or 18 in Elizabethan times to an average of 12.8 years today. Age-appropriate information about sexuality are vital to our daughters emerging as healthy, whole women. Given that for many girls puberty will start in their early teen years, we should start having conversations with them about sex and sexuality while they are young. We need to offer them alternative voices and role models of sexuality to those they are exposed to in the media and in pornography. This is especially important given that advertisers and broadcasters certainly will be targeting them with messages about sexuality long before their early teen years.

Please don't feel helpless or hopeless. Education works. We *can* help our daughters make sense of the mixed messages they are presented with.

Through my work, I meet girls and mothers who give me plenty of hope. I got to know a wonderful 11-year-old girl at a school I was at and also her mother, who completed one of Enlighten's courses for adults. The little girl was told by her dance teacher to start wearing not just full make-up for her concerts but false eyelashes, too. When her mother questioned why this was necessary she was told by the dance teacher that the eyelashes would increase her daughter's confidence. Mum and Ms Enlightened Tween both said no. As is so often the case, the dance teacher tried making Mum feel stupid: 'But all the other parents think it's fine.' When Mum investigated this claim, she found that four out of the ten dance mothers were also worried about the appropriateness of wearing false eyelashes but had been scared to speak out.

Whether you think the eyelashes were harmless or harmful is ultimately immaterial. What I love is that this little girl will not allow herself to be stretched and pulled into becoming a 'curvy, cool teen'.

She'll be a teen who will set boundaries, deconstruct all the mixed messages she'll be presented with and make choices she is truly comfortable with. She will not allow her sexuality to be shaped by misogynist music, plastic dolls, plastic women or the contemporary media environment, which would have her believe that to be hot she needs more make-up and fewer clothes.

She'll grow up on her own terms.

That is my wish for her. That's my wish for your girl, too.

That is what we all need to work towards.

Action plan

Talk to your daughter honestly and non-judgementally about sex and her own sexuality. Her school will provide information on personal development and sexuality, but she needs you to be involved in this dialogue, too. This is part of your core business in raising your daughter to become a happy, healthy woman. When is the right time to start? I had a very wise grandmother who used to say 'If a child is old enough to think of a sensible question, then they are old enough to hear a sensible answer.' Keep in mind, though, that the onset of puberty is a stage of development that will unfold over many years. There is no need to discuss *everything* all at once. Be guided by her physical and mental maturity level, and her interest.

Be prepared for a few awkward moments; I have found that older teen girls often try to shock by asking questions they don't think we will have answers for. ('So what is a 69'er?') If you respond calmly and in a matter-of-fact way, they are usually so impressed by your inability to be fazed that they go on to ask very thoughtful questions that really do matter to them. If you don't have an answer, be honest and admit that you don't know. It can be a powerful exercise to attempt to find answers together.

Be willing to try to resolve differences of opinion or at least be prepared to hear your daughter out, which will give her practice articulating her values. Encourage discussion by asking open-ended questions and actively listening to her.

It is vital to discuss the emotional component of sex, but think twice before making black-and-white statements such as 'Sex is only for people who really love each other.' Ideally, that might be true, but the reality may be quite different. Sex may be an expression of love, but it may also be an expression of boredom, curiosity, lust or even dark emotions such as anger or hate – for girls as well as boys. I have seen girls who engage in sexual acts only to later feel embarrassed by them. By helping your daughter to develop her emotional vocabulary, you will be helping her understand that sex not only has obvious physical consequences – pregnancy, STDs – but also an emotional impact. The glossy ads and catchy song lyrics rarely discuss complex human emotions. You should.

Get an effective internet filter.
None of the filters on the market are completely fail-safe but they do offer some protection from porn on your home computers. Limiting and banning access to certain sites is only one strategy, though. It is far more effective in the long term to discuss why these sites are not suitable and what your daughter should do if she stumbles across one.

Guide your daughter's media consumption.
Enter her world and work with her to make sense of it. The things that interest her can be tools to help you both explore

sexual stereotypes. Song lyrics, movies, television shows and teen magazines can all be excellent discussion starters. 'I find that when I read teen magazines I get a bit confused, as the advice offered can be quite contradictory,' says 14-year-old Lucy. 'It's like they might say in one article that there's no rush to worry about boys and in another they go on about how to tell if a guy likes you, or show girls looking all sexy with their boyfriends. I like being able to ask my mum what she thinks, too . . . it's not as embarrassing if I can show her an article and then start talking about it, as it is when I have to try to find a way of starting the whole conversation myself.'

Be a positive role model.
Have you bought into raunch culture? Have you accepted the myth that a woman is sexiest if she has porn-star fake boobs, and can channel her inner stripper? The 'girls gone wild' view of female sexuality is not always empowered or liberated. Have you ever noticed how vacant and bored most strippers look when performing? They are not aroused. They are often not even given real names. They are not some-bodies – just bodies. They exist only to please others. Why should women emulate this? If you clearly demonstrate a healthy and self-respecting sexuality, you'll be giving your daughter a good example to model herself on.

Reassure your daughter.
Let her know you think the media is trying to make girls grow up too fast, and that you find it unacceptable and will be working on stopping its impact on her. Girls I work with

love it when I tell them that I am mad as hell and I'm not taking it any more! They love to feel protected and tell me they are deeply comforted by knowing there are women who care passionately about their wellbeing.

Encourage your daughter to care about the issue.
High school girls are often furious when I show them inappropriate children's toys, and sexualised images and stories from tween magazines. In fact, at one school I worked at in Canberra, the 14-year-old girls spontaneously started booing when I showed an image of a Baby Bratz doll! I love this anger, as it shows me that though teenage girls may be too directly involved to instantly recognise the sexualising influences they are subjected to, they can clearly recognise what is unacceptable for their metaphoric (and literal) younger sisters. Harnessing this outrage will enable them to begin noticing more of the examples of adult sexuality being imposed on them.

Connect with other like-minded parents.
You might be surprised at just how many other parents share your concern over the sexualisation of children; you are not part of a moral minority! Make no mistake, outrage is widespread and mainstream. Join groups who meet in person or online. My blog (www.enlighteneducation.edublogs.org) can be a starting place, as it gives a voice to many parents who are worried about this issue. The Australian organisation Kids Free 2B Kids is dedicated to preventing children from being exposed to sexualised imagery, whether in the media, in advertising or at the toy store. At their website

(www.kf2bk.com) you can connect with others and find information on what you can do to help.

Speak up.
Write to companies that sexualise children and tell them to *back off*. Vow not to buy their products or services unless they change their marketing campaigns or pull inappropriate items from their shelves. Conversely, offer emails and letters of support to companies that keep it child-friendly.

Don't buy hyper-sexualised toys, clothes and other merchandise for your daughter or for other people's children.

Just don't, okay? No good can come from this.

Affirmations

I am in control of my own sexuality.

I set my own boundaries and my own terms.

4

Planet Girlfriend: The Highest Highs, the Lowest Lows

❧

How I loved my girlfriends when I was growing up. I still do love them but the need for their company and acceptance was so very *urgent* back then.

My childhood best friend, Janelle, was in my class throughout the last few years of primary school and right throughout high school, too. Remarkably, she retained her status as my best friend the whole time (apart from a few brief periods when she was relegated to Public Enemy Number 1!). We met when we were ten years old and I had just moved into a house in the next street from hers. She approached me on the first day at my new school and declared that as I had moved into her old best friend's house and we would now be neighbours, I would need to be her new best friend. She told me she would be over at 3.30 to play.

And we did not stop playing for the next ten years.

Our friendship was initially so simple. We shared a mutual love for collecting novelty erasers, starting secret clubs (I always ensured I was the captain) and riding our bikes. We also shared my younger sister Chantielle, who joined in all our adventures. Sure there was competition – over who had the most rubbers or who spent too much time talking to Chantielle – but it was all generally pretty uncomplicated.

By the time we hit high school, we were no longer simple little girls. Our interest shifted from exotic stationery to one-hit wonders The Electric Pandas, an Australian rock group whose one real hit was the song 'Big Girls'. The lyrics (that I knew for definite) included 'And now we are big girls . . . I remember the days when we thought our love would never die.' Sounded like an anthem for the sisterhood to me. I never quite knew what the other lyrics were, possibly something about 'Our faces break up' or was it actually 'We're gonna face this breakup'? As I was just starting to get pimples, I sang the former lyric – and loved the empathy I thought the lead singer, Linda Buckfield, showed not only for my love for my friends but also for my emerging spots.

The highest highs

Friendships between teen girls can be amazingly beautiful and authentic. Many girls deeply love their friends and these friendships provide a sense of belonging and acceptance that is sadly sometimes missing for them at home, where everyone seems to be so time poor and over-scheduled. I love the way girls giggle together, the way they play with each other's hair and cuddle, the way they can be so fiercely loyal and protective of each other. When I ask girls who it is that really knows them, understands them and loves them, the vast majority tell me it is their friends who make them feel these essential emotions of love and empathy.

A strong friendship can make you feel like you're floating, even in your darkest times.

Laura, 14

I love my friends so much. They really GET me. They understand me, accept and know me. I can be myself with them, which is a relief 'cause I am not always myself for others.

Meagin, 14

My friends are my safety. They've got my back. They won't let anyone disrespect me or hurt me and if I need anything — like, at any time — I just call them and they're there. I can call them at midnight, at three in the morning, whenever; it doesn't matter. We're just tight and that's it. They're my sisters.

Ricky, 16

I love my female friends because I can talk about anything with them. We can talk about things that I would never bring up with my mum.

Aimee, 15

Something that I love about my female friends is that no matter what, you can always talk to them and even when you are smiling they always know when something is wrong. Basically, without them there would be no way that I could live.

Carly, 16

Truth be known, the intensity of the love girls feel for their best friends threatens some of us mothers. It can be hard to all of a sudden feel less needed and to be the third wheel. *Why won't she go out with me any more?* we wonder. *We used to be so close, now she only ever confides in her friends.*

This, too, will pass. Just as there were things about your daughter's childhood that were emotionally rewarding – such as unconditional love and the feeling of being needed – there were challenges. The same is true for her adolescence. Your daughter still loves and needs you; she is just exploring what it feels like to love and need others, too. Her peer relationships now inevitably take on a much greater importance. Adolescence is also the time of emerging independence and this takes the form of moving away, coming back, moving away, coming back . . . Girls need a safe place to come back to and assurance that they are supported in their exploration.

The lowest lows

Janelle and I loved 'The Pandas' so much we even had their name embroidered on sloppy joes, which we wore everywhere. On the reverse, we labelled ourselves as 'Big Girls'. We now had a mutual desire to be older. And to be popular. Having lots of friends was visible recognition of our value. Having one close friend no longer seemed enough. We wanted *everyone* to love us.

How to acquire new intimate friendships? We both soon developed another hobby: collecting other girls' secrets. In high school, all girls learn that knowledge is power. We joined a wider circle of girls who were much cooler than we were. These girls were the 'A' group at our school: they were popular with the boys at the school next door and were slightly intimidating to the rest of us, as the leader was 'naughty'. Janelle and I knew instinctively that to maintain our position within this circle, we had to collect and disclose girl thoughts.

Once, Janelle joined the other girls in this group in forming a 'We hate Dannielle' club. I am not sure why I was on the outer that particular week (probably I had been too bossy; I confess that I did do a lot of bossing people about in my youth) but I do recall feeling deeply betrayed, sad and lonely. As we knew each other's secrets, my dark fears were used against me: 'You're a fat moll/slut/scrag.' Nothing worries a teenage girl more than being called fat or promiscuous. It didn't matter that the insults were groundless. I was a skinny, gangly creature and although I longed for a proper boyfriend, I was terrified of making actual contact.

I am certain that at other times, I would have betrayed

Janelle and delighted in attacking her weaknesses, the weaknesses that only I knew. If need be, we were prepared to betray each other to gain wider acceptance. When at war, nothing is off limits. We could, and would, turn on each other – viciously. Hell hath no fury like a teen girl scorned . . . by another teen girl.

And then the next week, we were all friends again. If anything, the friendship seemed heightened by the drama. Like lovers reunited after a fight, we basked in the warmth of our rekindled mutual affection.

The rules on Planet Girlfriend

This on-again-off-again, happy-and-now-sad, love-her-and-now-hate-her time for adolescent girls is governed by rules and codes that if you are an outsider can seem almost impossible to follow. Within girl world itself, however, the rules are generally well known and understood. Even when my friends collectively turned on me, I recall thinking that it was just the way of things, that it was simply my turn to be ostracised. I turned then to my 'B' circle of friends, a group of girls who were not quite as cool but were very funny and smart. In hindsight, they were girls I had much in common with and, better yet, they seemed to accept me flitting in and out of their world. This outer circle of friends had its own rules and when I dropped in to visit, it always took me some time to adjust to the new environment. I had to learn the native customs and reacquaint myself with the different dialect.

Although each girl group is in many ways a unique

continent of its own, there are always rigid rules: dress codes, rules about what behaviour is acceptable, and social rules that dictate whom the members can talk to and where they can sit in the school playground. Then there are the more flexible rules that may change within the group from day to day: rules such as what it is okay to eat, watch and listen to. If girls don't keep up with these rules, they can find themselves branded out of touch by their peers, engaging in something that is 'so yesterday'. As girls long for connection and belonging, keeping up with the rules is vital, exhausting work. In my 'A' group, failing to attend a sleepover was social suicide, because back at school on Monday you would be left floundering, unable to share the in-jokes or fully comprehend the new intimacies formed between group members.

Barbie bitches and cyberbullies

With its cliques, secrets, passive-aggressive exchanges and tears, teen-girl world can be a political, intense place. Unlike boys, who often get physical and then forget and forgive their differences, girls tend to ostracise their enemies and use words as weapons. This can be far more scarring and damaging in the long term. Many women I speak to still vividly recall the pain of being teased by other girls. And still feel guilt over the times they themselves teased other girls. Often, girls are bullied one minute and the bully the next, as they jostle for position within their social hierarchy.

The occasional falling-outs I endured were nothing compared to the daily attacks some girls are subjected to. As a teacher, I witnessed some truly devastating episodes of girl bullying. I have seen girls' lives made miserable by their peers. Often the reasons behind this victimisation are bewildering. One girl I met in my work with Enlighten sat scribbling furiously on her feedback form at the end of the workshop. And as she left the room, she hugged me – for a long time. Later, I read her comments, which included this poignant insight into her version of Planet Girlfriend:

> I learnt today that I am beautiful and I'm not ugly because they (the other girls at my school) might say I am. I'm not what people may say I am. I can imagine, I can love, I am beautiful, I also have purpose . . .

When I asked her teachers what this girl's experience of school was like, they told me that ever since she began high school she had been tormented: pushed down stairs, spat on, ignored. Why? The other girls all thought her ears stuck out. For this girl, there was no best friend to fall back on. For this girl, there was no 'A' group, no 'B' group. No opportunity to feel connected.

Girls' hostility can escalate into a systematic campaign of verbal and physical violence. Experts point to a new gang-like mentality among schoolgirls: to cement her position of power, a popular 'queen bee' gets her friends to bully or hurt other girls. 'Barbie bitches', a term to describe gangs of girls who believe they are beautiful, popular and have the right to intimidate those they deem less worthy, has became a frightening new part of our vernacular.

Technology has upped the ante on bullying and ostracising

behaviour. A study by a group of Australian academics found that as many as 93 per cent of school students had experienced some form of bullying via mobile phone, which they referred to as 'm-bullying'. The worrying thing about mobile phones is that children carry them all the time, increasing the likelihood and the impact of this form of bullying. The ability to bombard others with text messages or to pass on humiliating photos or videos is far greater than with older forms of bullying such as gossip and slander. M-bullying is immediate in nature; there is little time for the bully to reflect between keying in their message and hitting 'send'. A similar study claimed that 25 per cent of children in years 7 to 10 had experienced cyberbullying, that is, bullying via the internet. The anonymity of this kind of bullying means that children who may not be capable of being physical bullies can now actively participate.

Children generally don't like to tell adults they are being bullied, so we need to be very vigilant about what goes on in the schoolyard and behind our children's bedroom doors. Banning mobile phones and the internet is not the answer. We need to be more proactive in communicating with kids about the dangers of the always-switched-on world and give them strategies to deal with m-bullying and cyberbullying. This type of behaviour must be taken seriously by the adults who witness it and action must be taken.

Friendship 101

Keep in mind that adolescence is a stage, not a lifelong condition. The fact that an adolescent female's brain is rapidly developing helps explain some of the bad behaviour girls inflict on each other. This does not excuse nastiness and bitchiness. This must be acknowledged for what it is: unacceptable behaviour. However, it is vital to remember that although teen girls may look very adult, they are in many important ways still young children. We are all works in progress and teenagers especially so.

In adolescence, the brain undergoes dramatic changes. Many of these changes start occurring in late primary school and this is when teachers start to lament the sudden emergence of girl bullying and playground drama. The biggest changes relate to romantic motivation, sexual interest, emotional intensity, sleep regulation and appetite. There is also a general increase in risk-taking, novelty seeking and sensation seeking.

The frontal lobes of our brain are responsible for helping us to plan, consider, control our impulses, make good decisions and be empathetic. Studies into the brain development of teens have shown that their frontal lobes are not yet fully developed. Teenagers' brains 'are all tuned up for emotions, fighting, running away and romance but not so well tuned up for planning, controlling impulses and forward thinking', according to clinical psychologist Andrew Fuller.

When I was 14, a friend bit me on the arm one day, completely out of the blue. I ended up in tears, as she actually drew blood. When I asked her why she did it, she said she simply couldn't help it. I had just looked so delicious to her and she wanted to know how it would feel to bite me. She may have *looked* 14 going on 18, yet her impulse control was nonexistent; in many ways, she was just as impulsive as a toddler. It was this friend who was our 'queen bee', wild, reckless, exciting, hilarious. No wonder she was often in trouble at school; she had little self-control. Looking back, it troubles me that our teachers did not support her to make better decisions or give her strategies to cope with her whirl-wind emotions.

As a direct result of their stage of brain development, much of adolescents' behaviour is emotionally driven. For teen girls in particular, thoughts and emotions are more con-nected than at any other time. When you capture their hearts, their minds follow. This means that to help girls cope with friendship problems and become more resilient in the face of conflicts with friends, the best approach is to *empathise*, *emotionally engage* and *equip* them to make better choices. Empathy can be hard to muster because your daughter's fights with friends 'may seem so petty from an adult per-spective,' says Lisa Porter, the acting head of student welfare at Fairfield High School, in Sydney. 'It's so easy to say that it won't matter in five years' time, but five years when you're a teenager is a long time, and the social situation she is in really is her world. That world can feel like it's crumbling if things aren't right.' She urges parents to try to remember what it was like to be a teenager.

> *Arguments with friends can stuff up a whole day for me . . . If one of my friends treats me meanly, I feel guilty and think I have done something to offend them, which distracts me and stops me from thinking clearly at school.*
>
> Frances, 17

When you have positive relationships with your friends and family, it's a lot easier to succeed and be confident in what you're doing.

Nicola, 15

Lecturing your daughter on the need to treat others with respect will not work. Nor will simply demanding more socially acceptable behaviour from her. Girls may look as though they are listening and are receptive, but you will achieve little in the long term unless you give your daughter the skills she needs to make real changes. The development of healthy, fulfilling friendships is vital for girls' ongoing psychological and social development. But who shows girls how to navigate girl world? Where do they learn how to behave in their complex emerging friendships?

The soap operas they watch are full of drama, with interactions that are tumultuous, hostile and ultimately provide a negative picture of what constitutes relationships. The adult relationships around them may be unhealthy, too. I see women playing at cliques and passive-aggressive bullying even at my age. Some women and men play schoolyard politics indefinitely. Their brains have finished developing, so these adults do not even have the 'My brain's a work in progress' excuse to fall back on!

Girls need to be shown, by our example, how to relate to friends with empathy, love and respect. And we can go a step further and actively pass on some of the wisdom we have gathered through the years about making and keeping friends. In my work, I like to provide girls with solid friendship strategies. I go back to basics and take the time to teach girls how they can make friends. Isn't it startling that this fundamental task is something that people are rarely shown how to do? A sense of belonging is identified as one of the greatest needs of young people, particularly in the middle years of school. And the importance of friends, to us all, cannot be underestimated. As obvious as some of these pointers may sound, it's worth reiterating them to your daughter. It won't work if you sit her down and ask her to write these down or study them. Rather, look for opportunities to make the strategies relevant to her world.

Making friends

1 Introduce yourself and remember names. This shows people you have seen them and taken the time and energy to notice them.
2 Figure out who you want to be friends with and why. Your daughter will then be less likely to get caught up with friends who are not healthy for her.
3 Get involved in after-school activities. These will not only help your daughter learn new skills but it's also a great way for her to meet like-minded girls. She can try sports teams, debating, drama and so on.
4 Work on good conversation skills so you get better at listening and talking.
5 Be positive and upbeat. Girls might think it makes them look cool when they walk around saying how 'lame' things are but it usually just makes them look whiny.
6 Be sensitive to other people.
7 Take compliments politely and give them sincerely. This

is one many girls struggle with. I am always saddened
when I compliment a girl and she responds with 'Oh no,
I am not really . . .' or 'Yes, but I am hopeless at . . .'

8 Be willing to risk rejection. It is possible that someone
your daughter approaches may not be willing to make
a new friend and she needs to be prepared for the
possibility.

Once your daughter has made friends, what should she do
when things go wrong? And things will go wrong. Too often,
girls avoid dealing with issues as they are so determined to
be seen as 'nice' and nice girls don't make a scene. Yet often
all this repression does is allow ill feeling to fester.

News flash: it is normal to have disagreements and
fallings-out with friends. It does not mean we are unloved
or unvalued; it just means that an issue has arisen that needs
to be resolved. Sometimes the adults in teen girls' lives read
too much into their tensions with friends and unknowingly
validate the drama by discussing it at great length and counselling girls through matters they could easily deal with
themselves. A teacher of Year 6 girls told me she would end
up in tears over how unkind the girls, aged 12 to 13, were
to each other; she spent nearly all her lunch hour talking to
the various factions. Most of the arguments were over silly
things, she said, such as who spoke to whom, or who used
whose pencils. I couldn't help but think all the special talks
at lunch time in the teacher's office may actually have been
feeding this monster.

I doubt that a teacher would become as emotional over
boys arguing; their fights are more often dismissed as merely

'boys being boys'. Is it fair that we expect our girls to always be passive and nice? We need to equip girls with strategies to deal with conflict themselves. We need to accept that due to all the changes they are experiencing, in their brains and in their hormones, some anger is inevitable. And healthy! Conflict in fact prepares children for coping in the big wide world. If we mollycoddle them and don't teach them how to negotiate, solve problems and resolve conflict, we are setting them up to fail to cope with everyday adult life.

The 10 Steps to Conflict Resolution teach girls how to deal with conflict respectfully. They are based on the respect rules set out in the excellent book for teenage girls *Respect: A girl's guide to getting respect and dealing when your line is crossed* by Courtney Macavint and Andrea Vander Plimyn.

The 10 Steps to Conflict Resolution

1 **Plan ahead.** Teens tend to be impulsive. If they do not take the time to think about what they want to say to the person who has upset them, they may well say something they will regret or leave out a point they really did want to express.
2 **Don't put on a show.** It may be tempting for a teen to get other friends involved when they speak with the person who has upset them, but an audience will only escalate things, as everyone's emotions will be running high. A one-on-one conversation is always preferable, but if your daughter is really fearful about confronting the other girl, she may take a support person. This person should, however, be someone both girls feel

comfortable around, and their role is merely to be an observer. Note: it is highly inappropriate for you to be this person! More than once I have heard of a mother marching up with her daughter to confront a girl who has upset their precious child. This completely shifts the power dynamic of the exchange between the girls. Although it may be tempting to get directly involved, do not. However, if it is a serious matter such as bullying, discrimination or harassment, I do urge you to talk with the staff at your daughter's school.

3 **Home in on how you feel.** Using 'I' language – e.g. 'I felt hurt that you talked about me to the rest of the group' – is less likely to provoke than 'you' language – e.g. 'You can't be trusted.' Your daughter may not yet be very good at identifying her emotions. You can help her develop emotional literacy by offering a vocabulary to help her get in touch with her feelings. For example, 'Is what you're feeling really anger or is it betrayal?' or 'Are you scared? Threatened? Sad?' Brainstorm emotions with her.

4 **Admit your mistakes and apologise.** If your daughter feels that she is even partly at fault, in order to defuse the situation, often all the other person needs to hear is a simple, 'I was wrong, I am sorry.' A good apology should also include her saying what she is going to do to make amends or do differently in the future.

5 **Be specific.** Teenagers tend to generalise and exaggerate. It is rare that someone always does something we don't like. I encourage girls to clearly articulate exactly what upset them on this particular occasion and not to dig up

old wounds. 'I was hurt when after the party you told Melissa that I was no longer your friend' works much better than 'You always talk about me and this is just like what you did to me last year.'

6 **Offer time.** It is wise to offer the other person time to think, so that they do not speak impulsively. Your daughter could try saying something along the lines of 'I'd like to talk to you about what happened at the party as I'm feeling sad about how it ended. Can we talk after school, when you've had time to think about what happened, too?'

7 **Be calm.** Easier said than done! Teen girls can get very worked up when they are discussing friendship tensions. It is a good idea to teach your daughter some simple breathing and visualisation activities that can help her to stay chilled. You can find these in Appendix 2.

8 **Assert yourself.** As a teacher, I learnt very quickly the difference between assertive and aggressive. If you get aggressive with teens, they get defensive, angry and hostile. Rightly so! Rather, if your daughter wants other girls to listen to her, she needs to speak firmly and clearly, and show through her tone of voice and body language that she expects attention. Girls often begin sentences with unassertive phrases such as 'I may be wrong, but . . .' or use American pop-culture terms that detract from the power of what they are saying: 'It's kind of like . . .' or 'When you do that, I get sort of upset and stuff.' Encourage them to choose their words carefully and be strong in their dialogue. Give them

examples of assertive phrases they can use, such as 'I don't like it when you say/do that' and 'I expect you to treat me with respect.'

9 **Expect to be heard.** When your daughter approaches a friend to discuss something that is important to her, she has the right to expect that friend to stop what they are doing and listen. It is reasonable for your daughter to ask someone to put down their mobile phone or to stop looking at other things when she is speaking with them – unless she has picked a bad time to talk, in which case she should offer them time.

10 **End on a positive.** It is important to encourage girls to realise that they do not need to be friends with everyone. Some friendships do end. However, just because a friendship ends, it does not mean that the former friend now must automatically become an enemy. Assure your daughter that it is okay for girls to decide it is over and to simply move on – no longer friends, but still friendly. Also, friendships may end, but not forever. The friendship may just be 'over' for that week, or that term, or that year. Be careful not to engage in critiquing your daughter's past friend with her: if they make amends, your words may well be held against you!

The 10 Steps to Conflict Resolution are worth using in your own conflicts with your daughter, too. Often we adults throw respect out the window when we get upset. I have been known to turn into a raging banshee in the mornings, when I am getting my children ready for school. I have screamed at my ten-year-old daughter in front of her brother, telling her that she always makes us late, and I have then accused her of being a selfish person who always makes my mornings tough. In these moments, I feel as though my head might literally explode. I hate myself for being so ugly, but I hate the situation I am in even more, so I continue to rant.

I then spend the rest of the day feeling guilty.

And frantic school runs are just the smallest tip of the iceberg. I know that. My relationship with my daughter will need to be able to withstand so much more in years to come. With some solid strategies to fall back on, I believe it will.

Action Plan
Get to know your daughter's friends.
Not so you can join the gang, but so that you can gain an insight into the young people who are helping shape her. 'I run an open house of sorts,' says Lynne, the mother of two girls, aged 15 and 17. 'The girls' friends are always just dropping in. I love this as I have gotten to know all these little characters and have watched their friends grow into young women, too.'

Avoid passing judgement over petty things that her friends do. An example would be a comment such as 'Your friends all sound so silly when they say "It's kinda like" all the time.' Even if your observation is correct, your daughter won't like hearing you criticise her friends. Girls view their friends as almost an extension of themselves: when you criticise them, she may feel you are also attacking her.

Set limits.

If your daughter's friends practise or value behaviour that is unacceptable – such as taking drugs or binge drinking – then you should and must take a stand. Let your daughter know this is not acceptable. Impress upon her that you expect her to respect your opinions and behave accordingly. As parents, we have to set limits for our children. We are not supposed to be our daughter's best friend; we cannot enter the popularity contest that is being played out around her. As the parent, we must make the unpopular decisions if they need to be made.

The reality is, though, that it can be extremely difficult to break your daughter away from a peer group she is attached to, particularly as you cannot control what she does at school. In that case, it is worth examining why your daughter's friends are engaging in dangerous behaviour in the first place. Are they bored? Could you help them think of other things to do? Some girls just need their energy channelled into something healthy. If worst comes to worst and you feel you must ban your daughter from seeing a friend or group of friends, counter your sanction with something positive, such as helping your daughter connect with others by inviting a different group of girls over for a party or sleepover.

Elizabeth Broderick, Australia's sex discrimination commissioner and the commissioner responsible for age discrimination, tells me that when she and her sisters were teenagers, her mum 'was quite happy to set limits'. But to avoid having to give them a straight-out 'no' all the time, she would offer them a choice. 'And she was very crafty at this,' says Elizabeth. 'If we wanted to go to a party she didn't approve of she would simply organise another event the same night that was far more appealing; she'd orchestrate some grand adventure . . . At the time, we didn't realise what she was up to. We did what she had wanted all along, yet we grew up feeling in control.'

Get to know your daughter's friends' families, too.
Invite them over, especially if she is going to be spending time at their home. One of the wonderful things about forming connections with other girls' families is that you can share your experiences with other adults who are struggling with the same parenting issues as you. There is strength in numbers, too. Often teens try to make their parents feel as though they are the only ones who have a problem with what they want to do. ('But everyone else's parents let them!') Once you chat with other parents, you will soon realise that 'everyone else's parents' are also setting boundaries.

Widen her circle so your daughter can develop other friendships apart from those at school. That way, if things turn ugly in the playground, she will still have other girls she can connect with. Try external sporting clubs, drama or art classes, dance schools or organised groups such as the Girl Guides. Encourage your daughter to develop friendships with boys, too, and avoid teasing her about these. Many teen girls form genuine mutually fulfilling platonic relationships with boys. 'One of my closest friends is a guy,' says Kim, who is 15. 'I get annoyed when my parents tease me about this or imply there is more going on. There isn't. He is attractive, I guess, but to me – he is just my buddy. And he makes me feel understood. Things with him are often less complicated than with my girlfriends . . . There isn't the same sense of competition.'

It is important not to make the quest for friends a popularity contest. A few good friends may be all your daughter needs, so don't be concerned if she does not have loads of close friends.

Learn to distinguish a falling-out from bullying.
Your daughter may turn a temporary falling-out with a friend into a catastrophe and tell you everyone hates her and no one is her friend, when this is not really the case. On the other hand, she may actually be the subject of a real, ongoing campaign of bullying. If you have any concerns about your daughter's relationships with other girls, delve deeper. Ask her, sensitively and tactfully, listen to her closely and check with her school if you are still unsure.

Assess your relationships with your friends.
Are you still caught up in any toxic girl friendships? Do you have any friends who belittle you, dismiss you or make you feel ostracised? Or do you think you might be doing that to others? If so, it's time to free yourself of these patterns and choose healthier friendships – not only for yourself but also for the example you are setting your teen daughter.

Celebrate good friendships.
For many girls and women, girlfriends are some of the most important people in our lives. Isn't this why we big girls all fell in love with the show *Sex and the City*? Even those who

objected to the characters' rampant consumerism and preoccupation with finding male mates were ultimately seduced
by the show's celebration of the deep connection between
women. Forget Manolos and Big, what really resonated
was the friendships between the women. Let your daughter
know how important your girlfriends are to you and what
you value about them. Tell her how pleased you are when
you see her being a good friend.

Try to empathise with your daughter's strong feelings and
the emotional rollercoaster ride she is on. Don't belittle her
by telling her she is a drama queen. Try the 'Letter to my
teen self' exercise in Appendix 1 to reconnect with the feelings you had as a teen girl.

Listen.
You don't always need to solve her friendship problems for
her, but be there to hear her talk them through.

Affirmations

I surround myself with positive people and
attract good friends into my life.
I have compassion, I'm a good listener and
I choose my words carefully.

5

Drinks with the Girls

For a long time we thought [tobacco] was something
boys came to earlier and used more heavily and longer.
By the early 1990s, we'd seen an equalisation in the
tobacco use rates, with girls even sneaking ahead. We've
seen similar trends with cannabis use, and with drinking.
In a couple of decades, girls have caught up to the boys.

Professor George Patton, Melbourne's Centre for Adolescent Health

We are in the midst of a teen drinking epidemic. And
it is the girls who are overindulging the most. Studies reveal that girls aged 12 to 15 are more than three times
as likely as boys the same age to drink alcohol at least once
a week. Over 80 per cent of the drinking done by children
aged 14 to 17 is at risky levels that often lead to injury, for
when intoxicated young people are more likely to participate
in risky behaviour such as swimming, driving or fighting. It
takes a teen longer than it takes an adult to experience the
physical signs of intoxication. Teenagers do, therefore, tend
to binge, or drink to a more dangerous level, not realising

how drunk they are. Research shows that drinking alcohol during the teen years can interrupt key stages of an adolescent's development. A teenager's brain is also not yet fully developed for reasoning or thinking about consequences; it is far more finely tuned to respond to situations emotionally. Combine this with alcohol and you truly have a worrying cocktail. Many girls lament regrettable decisions they have made while under the influence.

Too many of our daughters are jeopardising their safety, health and their development; they are burdening themselves with hangovers and regrets. Why?

Attention, alcopops and escape

There is no one reason why anyone drinks, but in the many hundreds of conversations I have had with teenage girls about their binge drinking, some common threads have emerged.

In our hyper-sexualised culture, to gain attention increasing numbers of teen girls are adopting stripper-like dance moves and baring all when they go out with their friends. This is easier to do when girls are drunk and therefore less inhibited. How revealing are the song lyrics to the hit song 'I Kissed a Girl' by Katy Perry, in which she tells of kissing a girl even though she hadn't intended to: 'I got so brave, drink in hand . . .' It seems for Katy that the act of kissing another girl had more to do with alcohol – and a coquettish desire to provoke her boyfriend, mentioned later in the song – than any real pressing sexual urge of her own.

Teen girls tell me it is now almost passé to engage in a girl-on-girl kissing session in front of the boys at parties.

One girl told me: 'Getting smashed and then getting it on with a girlfriend used to be a guarantee of getting attention at parties, but now the boys expect more. They've seen it all before. Now they're like "Yeah, yeah, whatever."'

Girls also post their drunken antics on social networking sites such as MySpace and Facebook, or on YouTube, in the hope that they will gain instant celebrity status. It is no wonder that girls have grown to see alcohol as a way of getting attention, given how fixated we are with celebrities behaving badly. We voyeuristically feast on the alcohol- or drug-fuelled escapades of Paris, Britney, Lindsay, Amy Winehouse . . . We inadvertently glorify their train-crash behaviour by watching, fascinated, as these stars are carried out of bars and night clubs, or are forced into rehab. The trend among teen girls to publicise their drunken exploits has long-term implications for their lives. Just look at the media's and public's reaction to Paris, Britney and the gang: we may see them as celebrities but we also denigrate them as trash. Society is generally less forgiving of the 'fallen woman' than the 'man who likes a drink'. I cannot imagine that a male celebrity getting drunk, acting in an overly sexual way and passing out would capture the headlines in quite the same way as the female celebrities do.

Despite the headlines that scream 'raunchy', I do not think the paparazzi photos of drunk or drugged female stars look in the least bit sexy. Yes, they flash the right pieces of their anatomy; yes, they engage in the almost mandatory girl-on-girl grope – yet their eyes look glazed and bored. They are surrounded by hangers on, yet they look lonely.

Lonely and perhaps sad. Drinking can be a way of

self-medicating depression; bingeing is often a form of nihilistic escape. Ironically, as alcohol is ultimately a depressant, girls who drink to drown their sorrows end up feeling worse . . . and drinking more.

Girls also tell me they drink because they are bored. When drunk they feel more outgoing; and the uncontrollable giggling, toppling over and even making oneself sick is, they say, hilarious. And it can bring them closer to their friends, they argue. In girl world, you will do almost anything to fit in with your peers.

The alcohol industry has made a concerted attempt to appeal to young female drinkers' tastes, another possible reason we have seen a rise in the number of teen girls drinking. Prior to the early 1980s, the alcohol market included only beer, wine and spirits. Then ready-mixed drinks – RMDs, also known as alcopops – were introduced. Combinations of alcohol and fruit juices, flavourings and soft drinks, they were designed to appeal to new drinkers who did not yet find the taste of alcohol appealing. All that sweetness masks the punch. In 2008, Australian consumer group Choice got 78 teenagers (for legal reasons all aged 18 or 19) to do a taste test of soft drinks, alcopops, wine and beer. Though they could taste the alcohol in the wine and beer samples, when comparing the alcopops and soft drinks, one in four of the teenagers could not tell which contained alcohol.

With the introduction of alcopops, getting trashed became delicious. Whether a girl wants to drink to lose her inhibitions, to forget her problems or simply to be part of the gang, thanks to alcopops she can now do so without even having to taste the alcohol.

As a teen girl, at various points I drank for all the reasons above. It began at 14, when my friends and I would skol oh-so-sugary-sweet Passion Pop before underage Blue Light discos run by the local police. How the police that supervised these events never noticed that more than half the teens were blind drunk, I will never know. Most of us could hardly stand, let alone dance. Looking back now, what a sad sight we must have made. Young girls still dressed with pictures of Minnie Mouse on our shirts and jumping up with glee when our favourite song came on – smashed. We drank because everything became even more amusing. Falling over? How funny! Vomiting on your own feet? Hilarious! And we lost our social inhibitions.

I had my first proper kiss – with a boy I'd had a crush on for months – when I was drunk. I launched myself at him. He was drunk, too, so we sat together in a drunken embrace, no longer afraid of revealing that we liked each other. Nowadays, to really get his attention I would have had to provide him with a lap dance, too, but back then, a pash sufficed.

Later, as an older teen, I started to drink to dull my potential. My schoolgirl head ached with facts, figures, quotes for essays; it throbbed with a self-imposed pressure to be first, to be the smartest, the brightest. When I was drunk, I could barely string coherent sentences together, let alone formulate an argument. Being drunk was like taking a mind vacation.

For me, drinking seemed so grown up, just as it does to young girls today. Drinking is one of the marks of adulthood to most teens, who see the majority of the adults around them doing it. Alcohol features significantly in many elements of

Australian culture, from celebrations to commiserations. It is considered almost un-Australian not to have a beer.

In my house, my father drank from the moment he came home from work until he collapsed, asleep. While this wasn't very appealing to watch, strangely enough, to me it did look relaxing. And he became more cheerful and animated . . . until after the fifth or sixth beer, when he just became quiet. Or violent.

I felt quite rebellious engaging in an activity that seemed so adult and also so masculine. Largely as a result of watching my dad in his rages – which were thankfully infrequent but shocking and memorable nonetheless – I associated being drunk with power. I knew very few women who drank heavily. Certainly none of the women in my family drank; perhaps they may have had the occasional shandy, but I never saw them drunk.

It was almost as if being young women of the post-feminist age, we saw it as our right to indulge, too. If the boys could all get hammered, why couldn't we? Girl power!

Looking back at this stage in my life, I can see how dangerous my behaviour was. Being drunk did not really make me powerful. It made me vulnerable. My academic results suffered. I said things to friends I regretted the next day. I took stupid risks when drunk that I would never have taken sober: hitchhiking, crashing out by myself in rooms at wild parties, walking home alone, getting into cars with very drunk drivers. The fact that nothing truly serious ever happened to me was more good luck than anything else.

While drinking makes teen girls feel invincible, they are actually far more at risk when they are intoxicated. Their judgement is compromised; their reflexes are slowed; they are physically awkward. Young girls are at greater risk of violent and sexual assaults when they are inebriated. I am not blaming the victim: it is never her fault. But being drunk does make girls easier targets. We know that predators look for vulnerability, so girls are putting themselves at increased risk when they are intoxicated. Drinking is not so much a sign of liberation from sexism as a new form of enslavement for many teenage girls (and for many women, too).

What every girl should know about alcohol

Please take into account that figures are available only for men and women over the legal drinking age, 18.

Females are more vulnerable to the effects of alcohol than males. This is because males and females are physically different and so our bodies process alcohol differently. When a person drinks, alcohol enters the bloodstream and then, being water-soluble, it is distributed throughout the tissues of the body that contain water. Females usually have smaller bodies than males, which means that there is less water volume to take up the alcohol, leading to a higher concentration of alcohol in the bloodstream and a greater effect. This is compounded by the fact that fatty tissue does not take up alcohol and females have a higher proportion of body fat than males. With less alcohol-absorbing tissue in the body, a female will be more affected than a male who consumed the same amount. Additionally, the body's ability to break down and rid itself of alcohol is limited by the size of the liver and on average females have smaller livers than males.

The culture of dieting and striving to be thin also increases the impact of alcohol on females. Dieting leads to an excessive loss of body fluid and as it is the body's water content that takes up alcohol, there will be a higher concentration of alcohol in a dieter's system. This has serious implications for teenage girls.

Heavy drinking is risky for both males and females, but females are more prone to the acute and chronic effects of alcohol abuse. Because of our physical differences, the risk to our health starts at lower rates of alcohol consumption than it does for males. For women, the risk of premature death increases with more than two standard drinks of alcohol a day; at that point, the risk of death climbs to 40 per cent higher than it is for non-drinkers. For men, on the other hand, the risk begins to increase at four drinks a day.

The greater the amount of alcohol a person drinks above the guidelines, the higher their risk of premature death. Hence bingeing – consuming an excessive quantity of alcohol at once, a form of drinking adopted by most teen drinkers – is especially dangerous.

Because our livers are smaller than men's, women are vulnerable to liver damage and cirrhosis at lower levels of alcohol consumption. Alcohol increases a woman's risk of breast cancer and the risk rises with the level of alcohol consumed. A woman who drinks three or four standard drinks a day has a 35 per cent higher risk of breast cancer than one who drinks little or none. If a woman drinks more than four standard drinks a day, her risk is 67 per cent greater. Alcohol-related deaths in women usually take the form of strokes, injuries from falls, alcoholic liver cirrhosis and road accidents. Alcohol poses a further physical threat to women and girls in that it may increase their risk of being harmed by violence. Lastly, there is not only the risk of intoxication leading to unsafe sex and STD infecton or an unplanned pregnancy, but also the risks to the health of an unborn child.

Our dirty little secret

It frightens me that many parents seemingly dismiss their teen daughters' (and sons') drinking as just a rite of passage. I have spoken to many mums and dads who are almost hysterical about the possibility their teen daughter might start using drugs or have her drink spiked with drugs, yet are not at all concerned to hear she has been drinking alcohol. It is often parents who buy the alcohol for their teens; they allow the unsupervised parties; they lead the alcohol-goes-with-everything lifestyle, acting as drinking role models.

Concerned by the way adults in the community were turning a blind eye to students' drinking, St Peter's Collegiate Girls' School, in Adelaide, surveyed girls at the school about their alcohol consumption. They found that the most active time for underage drinking was during years 10 and 11, when girls range from 14 to 17 years in age. Parents often supplied the alcohol and girls found it easy to obtain alcohol, even from bottle shops. The most popular places to drink were at home, at a friend's home, at a party or in a park. The girls reported that the police didn't really trouble them about their underage drinking.

This school, which has set up an ongoing dialogue to

challenge community attitudes towards drinking, should be applauded for its honest, proactive approach. If we do not start to take teen girls' drinking seriously, we may be setting them up for a lifelong battle with the bottle. Research shows that teenagers, especially teen girls, who drink excessively are more likely to become alcoholics.

Beyond bingeing

The last day I drank alcohol was years ago, at my daughter's seventh birthday party. It had been a big day; as well as the kids, there were lots of adults over and, as always, lots of adults meant lots of booze.

I spent the next day lying in bed moaning and swearing – yet again – that I would stop drinking.

How many times had I had this conversation with myself? Was it really okay that here I was at 36, still wiping myself out?

My children, at ages five and seven, were surely becoming aware of the difference between adults who are sober and those who aren't. I wondered what they made of my drinking.

I did not start the day with alcohol and on weeknights I usually didn't have my first drink until the children had gone to bed. I never drank and drove. I had never needed a day off work due to being hungover. Most of my friends drank just as much as I did, just as frequently. Yet was downing a bottle of wine or more at each drinking session really okay?

No. I felt increasingly exhausted, both physically and emotionally. I was sick of looking for reasons to have a 'chardie' (how could something that sounds so harmless really be wrong?); disappointed in myself for never seeming to know when I had had enough; and saddened that in my bright, shiny life this 'drinking thing' was a part of me. It just did not fit with the strong woman I knew was my authentic self.

I sought out a GP I could talk to who could help me make better choices. I hadn't realised how much I relied on drinking until I was committed to stopping. The first few months were gruelling and there was surprisingly little support from some of my girlfriends, who were still drinking. 'Why stop completely?' 'How boring, Danni!' 'We won't be inviting you over for drinks and nibbles, then.'

But I knew I could never be a restrained social drinker. I never had been. It had always been all or nothing. Perhaps I have a genetic tendency towards drinking or maybe it's because I watched my father drink so heavily at home. What I do know for sure is that my dad's drinking completely destroyed his life: he lost his job and his family. I was not going to wait for the train to crash before I jumped off.

Our teenagers need us to be the voice of reason and control. This means that it is time for adults to end unhealthy drinking, too. Teens are targeted by campaigns against binge drinking but if you speak with them, they'll tell you that though some of their peers do binge drink, it's not fair that all young people are 'tarred with the same brush' and singled out. As Jennifer Duncan reported in Brisbane's *Sunday Mail*, binge drinking is 'a whole-of-community issue' and one we all need to take responsibility for if we are to resolve it. 'The first step in the binge drinking debate,' she wrote, 'is to acknowledge what young people are learning from our own behaviour and to adjust this behaviour accordingly.' Much has been made of the government's action plan to curb teen binge drinking. Yet sanctions will work only up to a point. We can limit the hours bars are open, tax alcohol and ban alcopops, but in the end it is up to us as parents to set limits within our own homes.

Promising news came out of the teen-drinking study conducted by St Peter's Collegiate Girls' School. It showed that girls are already well placed to learn new attitudes to drinking. The girls surveyed readily accepted people who did not drink alcohol, believing that they were free to choose not to drink. Across all year levels, the girls were well informed about drinking hazards such as binge drinking. The Year 12 girls felt very strongly about the role of parents in relation to underage drinking. These girls actually *wanted* enforced curfews and they did not want parents to turn a blind eye to their teens' drinking. Teenagers actually crave boundaries and limits because the pressure is then taken off them to make all the decisions.

I have seen girls drink but I don't. I think they look stupid, out of it. Girls just get smashed to impress other girls. I would never do that.

Rose, 13

An example of peer pressure actually being a positive force is that if you're at a party, there is always someone there that will say you don't have to drink or you don't have to smoke.

Brooke, 14

Drinking is really common in a small country town. It's like the only thing the other girls talk about all week at school – what they drank, how smashed they were, when they will drink next. I don't drink at all, which does make it harder to fit in, but I think drinking is just so stupid. If I have fun, I want to remember it after!

Lucy, 16

Action plan

Set a good example.

If your daughter grows up seeing you drink heavily and regularly, she is unlikely to take you seriously when you demand that she doesn't drink. I think many parents need to ask themselves some tough questions:

- Do I drink too much and too often around children, including teens?
- If so, what does my drinking teach them about how to socialise?
- What does it teach them about how to manage stress?

If you need to seek help to take control of your drinking, do so now. Don't wait for the train to crash; get off before things get ugly. Having quit alcohol myself, I know that it may seem like an overwhelming challenge – but you don't have to go it alone. In Appendix 4, Resources, you will find contact details for help, support and more information.

'I never saw my parents drunk and my daughter will never see me drunk,' says Elizabeth Broderick. 'We are what we do.'

Talk about alcohol honestly and openly.

There are a couple of great short films made by a young girl, Kylee Darcy, to dissuade other teen girls from drinking. The films won a competition in the United States that asked young girls to make Public Service Announcements that showed why underage drinking wasn't worth the adverse consequences. Darcy's films portray two teen girls who become ostracised by their peers, are thrown off a sporting team and get busted by their parents when a video of one of them drinking at a party surfaces on a social networking website. A good way to get a dialogue going with your daughter is to watch the films with her at www. alot2lose.com.

You can ask questions such as these – in your own words – as a starting point for a meaningful talk:

1 Have you ever seen people acting in a way they wouldn't normally, because they were drunk? How did it make you feel?

2 As well as the social risks of drinking, what physical dangers are there in drinking too much? In what ways does it make girls more vulnerable and exposed?

3 What can you do to reduce these risks for you and your friends?

4 If you saw friends acting in a way that makes you anxious, what would you do? What could you do to take control of the situation?

5 Do you think that these films get the message across about why it's bad to binge drink? What would make them more effective or relevant to you and your friends?

Set standards and stick to them.

I do not believe in the argument that it is better for parents to buy alcohol for their teens and let them drink at home. Parents who take this approach say that it is preferable because at least this way the teens can be supervised, and that otherwise, the teens would just go and get alcohol themselves anyway and may binge even more.

This is a widespread opinion. But if you currently agree with it, please consider this: if your daughter is determined to try marijuana, will you go and score some for her, too? The parallel may seem extreme as, unlike alcohol, pot is illegal. But remember, underage drinking is also illegal, whether inside or outside the home. I think it is a slippery slope once you start condoning acts that are illegal and unhealthy. And your teen will use your compliance against you later: 'Why can't I go to the over-eighteens gig? You let me drink here anyway so what's the big difference?'

Contrary to popular belief, taking a stand on drinking will not drive your teen to sneak out and get trashed more often. In fact, research shows that when parents allow their children to drink at home, it normalises drinking and lowers the children's inhibitions to drink more. Studies also show that the longer we postpone our children's introduction to drinking, the smaller the risk that they will develop long-term problems with alcohol.

Say no. Make a stand. It may be hard to enforce, yet even if your daughter does break your rule, at least you will both know you didn't condone her drinking. Don't make it easy for her.

Action plan

Offer alternatives.

Encourage your daughter to get involved in special underage drug- and alcohol-free events.

Be calm.

If your teenager does get drunk, try not to overreact as this may make her feel that she can no longer confide in you. Ensure that she is physically looked after by increasing her fluid intake, as she may be dehydrated. When she's sober, explain you're disappointed and work through with her the reasons why you do not want her drinking:

- It is illegal.
- It is damaging to her health.
- It will affect her sporting and academic performance.
- She may do things under the influence of alcohol that she will be embarrassed about later.
- Drinking will increase her risk of being harmed.

Affirmations

My body is a temple and I honour it by making
good, healthy choices.
I seek healing, healthy ways to relax and
enjoy myself.

6

Shopping for Labels . . .
or Love?

❧

When I was little, I fancied growing up to be a lawyer. I could picture myself standing up in front of a packed courtroom, everyone listening, rapt, as I upheld justice. As it turned out, my calling in life turned out to be standing not in front of judges and juries but in classrooms, talking – and perhaps more importantly, listening – to young people. When I talk to them about what *they* want to be when they leave school, for many it is not a question of choosing a profession such as lawyer, doctor or teacher. It is about money and fame. At high-school level, I have heard the refrain: 'Don't care what I am, Miss, as long as I make money, hey?'

In primary school, I have seen girls between six and seven years old who have goals such as 'be famous', 'be a model', 'be on TV', or even 'be pretty, famous and maybe a singer and actress'.

Wanting to be a successful businesswoman or skilled professional, or to excel as an artist or entertainer, is a worthy goal. I am inspired when I see entrepreneurship and ambition in girls, because I know the freedom and sense of personal fulfilment that success in a business or career can bring. What worries me is the vagueness and blind materialism of wanting just to 'be rich' or 'be famous'. The message girls are being sent is that the only measures of success that truly count are fame and wealth. Not fame and wealth as a result of a specific skill, talent or course of study, but a general aura of fame and wealth.

We can see the seeds of this in reality TV shows that turn ordinary people who can kind of sing or are almost models into insta-celebrities dripping in cash prizes and endorsement deals for major brands. We can see it in glossy magazines that zone in with forensic accuracy on the latest hot designer must-have bag, jeans, mobile phone, party dress, boots, necklace or exotic pet the insta-celebrities are all being snapped with by paparazzi. Fame, wealth and branded luxury products have fused into a great big seductive orb that many girls are attracted to like moths to a flame.

The current generation of children has been found to be the most brand-aware in history. The average teenager in the United States has 145 conversations about brands each week. In the UK, almost half of children surveyed said that the only kind of job they want when they leave school is one 'that pays a lot'. In Australia, children aged 10 to 17 have 'more money, more toys and more things to spend their money on than ever before', according to the YouthSCAN national survey, which takes the pulse of the country's young people every two years. It is not uncommon, the survey found, for a teen to own their own mobile phone, mp3 player or iPod, DVD player and digital camera. These acquisitions of course come on top of fashion, accessories, cosmetics and the cost of going out with friends.

Why should we be concerned about this? Because along with heightened consumerism, adolescents are taking on some very adult-sized burdens. Australian teens are working and earning more than ever before and a significant number are suffering stress from owing money to credit card companies, mobile phone carriers, and friends and family. They are even beginning to show signs of something you may be familiar with as an adult: 'choice fatigue'. That's when you become overwhelmed by the vast array of consumer products you seemingly *must* make a selection from. More and more kids wish that the whole consumer merry-go-round would just slow down for a second. Researchers have even found that when a child is more materialistic, she tends to be more depressed and anxious and have lower self-esteem.

We should be concerned, too, because teenagers now account for such a big chunk of the consumer market that they are ferociously targeted by marketing and advertising campaigns. While our daughters are still learning, growing into adults and forming their own identities, they are especially vulnerable and impressionable consumers, and marketers know that. You can't help but feel a chill when you read the words of one marketing professional who said at a big marketing and advertising shindig in New York: 'Kids are the most powerful sector of the market, and we should take advantage of them.' Can you think of any circumstance where it's okay for the words 'kids' and 'take advantage of' to be linked? Me neither.

Right about now you might perhaps be bracing yourself for a sobering anti-consumerist spiel. But my aim isn't to make you or your daughter feel bad about getting a kick out of shopping, or to make you feel guilty for lusting after that cool new phone or cute handbag. Don't fear: I am certainly not about to give up the occasional shopping splurge. I'm not saying that shopping and spending money is *all bad*. What I am saying is that for our sakes and our daughters' sakes we should take a minute to look more deeply into what motivates our spending and what influences our attitudes towards money.

It's okay to want that designer bag, but let's unpack it . . .

Designer-label armour

When I was a teenager, girls tried to distinguish themselves from the older generation. This is one area where life for teen girls is different today than it was when we were growing up: now the two of you may well be scrabbling to snatch the same handbag in the sales. You might borrow each other's belts. And something may happen that would have been totally alien to our mothers: your daughter might occasionally heed some of your fashion tips.

More and more, young girls are aspiring to wear labels and serious fashion designers that were once associated only with grown women who read *Vogue*. At the same time, more grown women are gravitating towards those same hot designers and where once your average woman may not have known a Manolo from a Christian Louboutin, today she and her daughter may both be luxury-brand literate. The dividing line between what is fashionable for mothers and daughters has become blurry; there is an overlap in the products both groups covet.

My mum loves fashion also, and knows heaps of new styles before I do . . . I often borrow my mum's clothes; I also ask her opinion on what I am wearing a lot, too. I like going shopping with my mum just as much as I do with friends, since we have very similar tastes in clothes and like shopping at the same shops, as well as liking the same labels.

Paris, 14

That it's important to me to buy certain clothes, shoes, bags, phone, etc. – my mum is very understanding with that sort of thing. And I love her for it. I like going shopping with my mother because I love spending time with Mum! She's the best thing in the world.

Renee, 15

Me and my mum have similar tastes in fashion, so it makes shopping a lot more fun because on the rare occasion that we have a shopping day, we go to the same store.

Maddi, 16

For teen girls, the aim is to look more sophisticated, while for us the goal is to look youthful. Clothes, shoes, bags, cosmetics, lotions, hair-care products, sunglasses and bling – many teens use this cluster of products to craft a more adult, worldly look. With the same products (plus a stash of anti-wrinkle serums) we do the reverse: we aim to look young and hip. Many teen girls want to look like they're in their twenties, powerful, savvy, in-the-know, sexy and rich. So do many of their mums. And this look does not come cheap. At the very least, it has to *seem* like it took a celebrity's salary to achieve it.

Rose, a 13-year-old girl I know through my work who happens to be naturally stunning, told me it takes her just over an hour to get ready for school each morning. 'I have a shower, then put on my make-up, blow-dry my hair and then straighten it . . . I wear mascara, eyeliner, lip gloss, moisturiser for my face and legs, glitter on my eyes – like, if it is a special-occasion day – deodorant and body spray. I have done this since Year 7, when I was 12.' As she told me this, it struck me that the process Rose was describing was like a warrior preparing to go to battle, slipping on her armour, piece by piece, until she feels strong and powerful and ready to go out and face the fight. Many grown women perform a similar ritual at the start of each day. It is something girls and women do to feel strong and in control. Just as the women in *Sex and the City* express their prestige, power and sexuality through shoes and handbags, perhaps that is what many of us are attempting to do, too. Women and girls are armour-plating themselves, outwardly expressing independence, strength and a kind of don't-mess-with-me attitude.

Marketers capitalise on the urge teen girls have to feel

independent by infusing 'girl power' into their products. The term is used so often to sell things to girls (and women) that it has become virtually meaningless. Australian cosmetics guru Napoleon Perdis uses girl power to sell, of all things, a lip gloss. Apparently, it is 'The Ultimate Girl Power in a Gloss'. There is actually an entire brand, Girl Power Beauty, marketing skin and hair-care products to tweens. How about a cute little T-shirt with giant glossy supermodel lips and the words 'Girl Power' emblazoned across the bust line? You can order one online now.

Marketers and department stores love it when we equate certain bags and shoes, or outward qualities such as looking fashion-savvy and hip, with female strength, independence and, ultimately, happiness. But all those women in past decades who fought against gender inequality didn't do it just so we could live by a new anthem: 'I am woman, see me shop.' Surely the real reason we want equal pay for women is not simply so that we can spend it on more stuff . . . *beauty* stuff. As Jennifer Thomson wrote in her British blog 'The F word', '"Girl Power" is feminism, but feminism by marketed, picture-perfect, precise numbers.' She was writing about the original girl-power group, the Spice Girls, whose success showed that our marketing-laden culture likes 'to turn people into things. The inventions of Baby, Sporty, et al, stripped away the person to leave behind a commodity.' Victoria Beckham and her husband, David, embody this. Open any glossy mag and you will probably see one of them gazing out, imploring you to buy perfume, underwear, shoes, clothes. Posh, one of the original icons of girl power, has, along with Becks, become a living brand.

For girls and women alike, marketing messages can be very seductive, as can the pictures we see splashed everywhere of the rich, famous and powerful packaged head-to-toe in brand-label products. It may seem that we will be empowered if we buy those products. They promise to signal to the world that we have prestige and status, and that we are desirable and should be taken seriously. But real girl power is not about buying products. *Things* don't make us powerful. Deep down, I think we all know that isn't clothes, bling and the latest mobile phone that can truly make us feel happy and in control. Only we ourselves have the power to do that.

Standing out, fitting in

Teen girls feel a strong need to carve out their own identity. They want to be and look like individuals, with their own style and image. Yet at the same time, no teenage girl wants to be on the outer or to be perceived as uncool or clueless about what's in. They want to be part of a group; they have a genuine and valid need to fit in with friends and peers. You may remember treading a fine line yourself in your high school years. If you were too slavish a follower of the latest fashions you looked like a try-hard; on the other hand, if you were wearing the wrong shoes you risked being relegated to the outer reaches of the girl-world galaxy.

The people who sell products to our kids are only too aware of this eternal teenage paradox. Owning the right brands and products – and putting them together in her own style – is one way that a teen girl can walk that razor's edge between being in and being out. Following a brand enables girls to associate with a group: the other kids who gravitate towards those brands. The labels and products a girl displays can be like a social code, offering up signs of what kind of girl she is and who her tribe is. For instance, a Ralph Lauren top, Tiffany charm bracelet and Burberry bag sends out one signal. Vans sneakers, Roxy cargo pants and a Billabong T-shirt – a whole other signal. The importance of the social aspect of clothing can be seen when girls go shopping: they like to shop in packs. When a girl holds an item up to her friends and asks 'What do you think?' she's second-guessing her own taste and testing whether it fits in with her tribe's.

In our marketing-saturated culture, product ownership has joined the list of factors girls use to rank each other socially: to a girl's beauty and popularity we can now add the rating of how fashionable and prestigious the stuff she owns is. American author Alissa Quart investigated the world of teen marketing for her eye-opening book *Branded: The Buying and Selling of Teenagers*. What she noticed during her research was that the girls who owned the most name-brand products tended to be those who struggled to fit in according to the standard criteria girls judge one another by: they had an awkwardness about them or weren't conventionally attractive. 'While many teenagers are branded,' she writes, 'the ones most obsessed with brand names feel they have a lack that only superbranding will cover over and insure against social ruin.'

The frenzy for wearing the right labels reaches hysteria point around Year 10 and Year 12 formal time. In the lead-up, a girl's list of what she needs for the big night can become the teen equivalent of a bridezilla's: the right designer dress (actually, two dresses: one for the formal, another for the after party), jewellery, handbag and shoes, professional hair and make-up, tanning, waxing, buffing and sufficiently glamorous transport to get them there, stretch Hummers being a particular favorite. The total cost is generally well over a thousand dollars.

Parents often don't mind shelling out for just one night in their teenager's life, with some mums getting almost as excited about it as their daughters. When most of us were at school, formals weren't such a big deal and if any girls were wearing designer dresses, we probably didn't realise. Having missed out on the hoopla, it seems that plenty of mothers are happy to spend up big so they can vicariously experience it through their daughters. This only fuels the competitive madness of it all. At one high school, a girl bragged to me that her mother had flown her *to Paris* to buy her formal dress. I was speechless when, in the next breath, she revealed that there was a down side: as it was a Parisian label, only diehard fashionistas would know the designer, so she would have to explain to the other girls how prestigious her dress was.

If they harnessed all the energy they spend on what they'll look like on formal night, think of all the other great things girls could achieve; they could probably light up a major city. The national franchise director of Prom Night Events, a Sydney-based company that organises school formals, said, without irony: 'If you ask the average 15- to 18-year-old what is more important to them, the formal plays equally as much on their mind as the HSC [final exams], if not more.'

That kids feel products make a contribution to their self-esteem, identity and social success is borne out in studies, such as one in which 62 per cent of adolescents aged 12 to 13 said that 'buying certain products makes them feel better about themselves'. More than half of the same children felt pressured to buy particular clothes or CDs because their friends had them. In a way, it is as if marketers and advertisers that target teen girls are selling not handbags, make-up or mobile phones, but the promise of friendship and a sense of belonging.

When you look at the way brands are sold, companies approach it from the angle of creating a whole lifestyle around the brand. Designer fashion labels do not stop at clothes. There are the handbags, purses, shoes, sunglasses, watches, earrings, pendants, rings, gym gear, key rings, mobile phone bling, perfume, body sprays, room scents, homewares, and on and on it goes. Their TV ads feature gorgeous, sexy, fulfilled-looking young people just hanging out together laughing (or scowling fashionably, depending on the brand) and at the end you wonder, 'Hang on, what product are they selling?' It's not so much a product you are being sold as a feeling. Girls and women are encouraged to feel a positive emotion – a sense of belonging, perhaps – when they see the brand's label. It's not that the handbag bearing this particular label is really all *that* different to any other handbag in the shops at the same time. They both do the same job: carrying your stuff. It's the emotion, the lifestyle, the identity associated with the label that makes someone want to buy that particular handbag.

If a company can capture a teen girl early on, can make her associate herself and her lifestyle with their brand, they have a friend – oops, customer – for life. As Alissa Quart writes, 'teenagers have come to feel that consumer goods are their friends – and that the companies selling products to them are trusted allies.' Marketers openly admit that pushing a brand is all about giving the shopper a positive emotion and a sense of being connected not just to the brand but to the entire lifestyle and community the brand represents. The message used to be that you should buy a designer-label product because it was an assurance of quality. That has changed. Now it's all about 'the "image" the label represents', according to global research company Nielsen.

Celebrity endorsements play a big role in selling products because fans want to belong to the same club as their favourite star. The celebrity makes the brand a star and, by extension, a person who buys that brand feels they have become a little bit of a star, too. When I ask teen girls about their ideal job, quite a few say 'celebrity stylist', perhaps in the mistaken belief that it equates to 'celebrity BFF' (best friend forever). They fantasise that an average day at the office might consist of conversations like:

'You look so hot in that dress.'

'Shall we try Prada next?'

'Do you want to go get a latte?'

An increasing number of girls also nominate celebrity fashion icons as their role models. 'She's my role model, I love her style,' a girl might say of Sarah Jessica Parker or Jessica Alba, for instance.

The twist is that the cashed-up celebrities decked out in designer labels rarely have to pay for them; they are showered with the stuff by fashion houses and sponsors who know that their largesse will translate into sales. Most of the profits made by the big labels come not from sales of high-end couture garments but from selling the dream to average girls and women willing to spend a bit extra on perfume or undies that bear the designer label.

I wouldn't say it is important to own designer labels, usually because nobody else really knows if it's designer or not – however, I am not going to lie, I love my designer labels. I feel the quality of the clothes is better and lots of designers have their own cool style. Karen Walker, for example, has amazing clothes, ones I would struggle to find cheaper versions of somewhere else.

I once saw lots of pictures of celebrities holding a type of phone and automatically really wanted one. It was nice, expensive and wasn't compatible with my mobile phone network but since heaps of celebrities had it I thought it was cool. People who see something on a celebrity . . . suddenly think it is a thousand times better than if they saw it in a shop window . . . it is the person who is wearing or holding it that makes them want it.

Paris, 14

As much as 'it's what's on the inside that counts', I still feel it's nice to know you have the latest clothing, etc. – although I don't get upset if I'm not 'up with the latest fashion' because I like to be an individual.

Renee, 15

What mums and dads don't realise is that even though we are happy with ourselves, we as girls feel that if we don't have all the latest clothes we will not fit in and not be comfortable in our own skin.

Maddi, 16

What is a label worth?

I travel around the country and meet girls from all along the social spectrum. What I have found is that girls from more comfortably well-off homes tend to be the least interested in labels. In fact, some will prefer to look for cool op shop finds, to enhance the individuality of their look. That is because these girls are already perched at the top of the social ladder and have the least to prove to their peers. The greatest pressure is felt by those who have the lowest disposable income. Ironically, it is girls who can least afford them that have the greatest social need to display prestige brands and products. For them, the right brands can feel especially important to their sense of worth.

By continually stressing to them that in order to *fit in* they need to *buy in* to their labels, companies are placing unfair stress on the least wealthy. As adults, most of us have experienced status anxiety at some time. We have felt the pressure to 'keep up with the Joneses'. Some teen girls feel the same way and are just as worried as their parents about having enough money and maintaining their social status. The cure for this anxiety? According to advertisers and marketers, it would seem that the solution is to go shopping for yet more brand-label products.

If a girl is unable to afford the brands she has been told

will make her desirable, sexy and 'worth it', what is she supposed to do? I have met countless teen girls who will scrimp and save and do without all sorts of necessities just so they can buy a particular product. Perhaps the longing for branded self-worth is also partly why we have seen an explosion in the market for counterfeit designer-label products. Everyone wants to buy into the dream and this is the only way some of us can. I don't feel too sorry for the huge corporations when they cry foul about fakes – after all, they created the consumer lust. It could be argued they have fallen victim to their own marketing campaigns.

More worrying is the fact that some girls and women are willing to do whatever it takes to get the designer labels they want. Theft is a tempting way to get otherwise unattainable luxury goods. Using one's body as currency is another. To a certain degree, girls have been primed to see the latter as socially acceptable. When a man showers a woman with expensive gifts, he's deemed to be a catch, and friends and family will urge the lucky woman to snap him up. If she gets engaged to him, the first words she's likely to hear from other women are 'Let me see the rock!', as if her worth as a person is measured in carats. These may seem like harmless examples, but I think we see their echoes in the very real and very disturbing instances of teenage girls giving in to sexual pressure from guys who promise them designer handbags or shoes.

Beyond the brand

Some of the intangible things teen girls especially crave – a feeling of belonging, of admiration and acceptance, and

125

of connection with others – are what designer labels and department stores are really promising to deliver, not just jackets and perfumes and iPods. Perhaps many mothers are also craving these things.

When we go shopping, are we and our daughters really searching for a sense of belonging, a sense of community and a feeling of self-worth that we aren't finding in day-to-day life?

Are we building up our armour on the outside because we feel as though there isn't enough substance underneath?

The advertisers' and marketers' promises of a better life through products are just an illusion, of course. Like many women, you may remember a time when after a trip to the local shopping centre for some retail 'therapy' you found that you arrived home feeling strangely . . . empty. That's your inner voice telling you that shopping can meet only some of your needs. For deeper feelings of connection and self-worth, we need to look for something more real, more lasting. Most of the time, when we go shopping we set out in the belief that buying things will make us happier. There is evidence, though, that the pressure on us to buy more and more products can end up making us *less* happy. Just as Dorothy's friends in *The Wizard of Oz* discovered that the Wizard was all smoke and mirrors and they would have to look within themselves for the qualities they sought – intellect, emotions and courage – we need to look beyond advertising and marketing wizardry to find what will make us genuinely happy and whole.

As parents, we may feel an additional pressure when it comes to buying for our children, because their desperate longing for an array of products seems so pressing. Especially when they are too young to work or they want a big-ticket item, girls can beg in the most heartfelt way for products they 'need – like, really, really need, right now'. And it can be difficult to judge the difference between a teenage girl's want and need, because we know how important it is for girls to feel that they belong, that they are 'in', not 'out'. This is a judgement call that really only you can make, as you know your daughter best. One point to consider, though, is that while advertisers and marketers will try to tell you that their products can meet every need, your daughter's most fundamental needs, the ones that will prepare her for adult life, cannot be met in a store. Self-esteem, ethics, values and attitudes – these are developed primarily at home, so parenting that offers both affection and limit-setting is much more important than having a bank balance big enough to buy your daughter everything she wants.

Some researchers in this field believe that corporations take advantage of the fact that many young people feel a void in their home life because parents are spending more and more time out of the house working (so they can afford to buy things for their family!). They say that it is easier for merchandisers to capture the heart and mind of a teenager who doesn't have a robust home life, because she will be looking elsewhere for roots. It's no wonder then that girls I've spoken to say one of the things they like best about shopping trips with their mums is simply the chance to spend time together. Sixteen-year-old Steph speaks for a lot of girls when she says, 'I don't really go shopping with my mum all that often, about once a month, but when we do go shopping it's good because we both get to catch up on things.' Shopping with your daughter and sharing fashion tips can be a great, fun way to bond with her. The important thing is to know that even if you can't afford to buy her all the latest products, you can give your daughter far more important things that she can't purchase in any store.

A man is not a financial plan

Consumerism will no doubt be a feature of our culture for many years, if not generations, to come, so financial planning is paramount. The global credit crunch was also a stark reminder of the need for financial savvy. And due to our aging population, when our daughters reach retirement age, it is forecast that governments will be unable to afford a pension system on the same scale as today's. All of this means that now more than ever, we should be providing teen girls with a good financial education. Yet what many teenagers are entering adult life with is not an understanding of personal finance but debt. Almost 10 per cent of people who went bankrupt in Australia in 2007 were only 15 to 24 years old. The same age group accounted for over 20 per cent of people who signed debt agreements, an alternative to declaring bankruptcy.

Many of the young people who are in debt report having a high level of stress about it. The highest stress level is among those who owe money to credit card companies: in the YouthSCAN survey in 2007, almost half of them said they were anxious about it. Mobile phone bills run a close second when it comes to financial stress for teens. A spokeswoman for the New South Wales government's Office of Fair Trading said financial counselling services have 'young people in their late teens, early 20s, suggesting they should become a bankrupt because they have racked up thousands of dollars in premium services on mobile phones'. Fees for premium services – downloads, ringtones, voting on reality TV shows, competition entries – can snowball without your daughter realising. The true cost is often buried in ambiguously worded print that seems to have been sized for ants to read.

What makes this especially galling is that companies sell premium services by playing directly on teen girls' insecurities. Flip to the back of a teen-girl magazine and you'll see ads for mobile phone wallpapers that are mostly variations of the 'Don't cha wish your girlfriend was hot like me?' theme. Your daughter can also download a wallpaper featuring the picture of a hunk from *Home and Away*, or an anonymous young shirtless guy with ripped abs. There are ads for SMS chat services offering her the opportunity to chat and flirt with hundreds of guys. Then, when the pressure to be hot and sexy has got too overwhelming, she can consult an internationally renowned, guaranteed 99.9 per cent accurate love psychic via SMS, so that the future looks clearer to her.

Here we are with this relatively new technology at our disposal and it is being used to recycle tired old ideas of what a girl's future happiness should consist of: being hot and sexy, and getting a guy. Another stubbornly persistent idea is that a girl doesn't need to worry about her financial future, because a knight in shining armour will one day come along with enough cash to pay off the mortgage and ensure a comfortable retirement. Despite all the advancements that have been made in gender equality, there are girls – and grown women – who do still hold on to this dream. Too many teenage girls tell me it doesn't matter what they want to be when they leave school, because they'll 'marry a rich man anyway'.

The truth is, our girls need to grow up to be financially independent women.

I stress the importance of financial independence to all young women. As I say to my daughter, Lucy, a man is not a financial plan!

Elizabeth Broderick, Sex Discrimination Commissioner and Commissioner responsible for Age Discrimination

I have made two saving accounts so that half of my pay goes into one and the other half into the other. One saving account is for me to use just for things such as going to the movies with friends or clothes or food, etc. The other account is locked so I cannot get any money out of it unless I go into the actual bank. The money in this account is my savings for the future.

My friend had set up two accounts and I thought it was a good idea so I asked my parents about it and they let me do it, too.

Steph, 16

I do save money for the future; I think it's very important so that you have some funds so if an emergency crops up it's

*there for you. My parents set it up for me when I was two
years of age. Therefore I just grew up with it, was encouraged
to save my whole life.*

Renee, 15

Action plan
Maximise the mobile phone plan.
One of the easiest ways for teenagers to rack up large debts
is through their mobile phones, which for many girls almost
seem to have become bionic extensions of their own hands.
Teenage girls need to talk and express themselves to their
friends, so nagging them to stop using their mobiles will
only be counterproductive. But being clever about the plan
you sign your daughter up for can help to keep her bills
manageable. You may remember the story of the 13-year-
old Californian girl who sent 14,528 text messages in one
month, ending up with a bill 440 pages long. Her rate of
text messaging – one SMS every two minutes during every
waking hour – was totally over the top, but at least this
girl's parents had her on the right plan, one that allowed
unlimited texting! Using the mobile company's plan to your
daughter's advantage – now, that is smart. Setting limits is
smart, too. The girl's parents set a new rule: no texting after
dinnertime.

Cut the credit card.
Getting a credit card at an early age can be a terrible burden
to your daughter, as it may be many years before she earns a
high enough wage to dig herself out of a debt hole. Instead

of saving for the future, she may instead be paying off outfits long out of fashion and consigned to the back of the closet. There are parents who opt to co-sign so their teen can have a credit card. Think very carefully before you get into such an arrangement, as you will be responsible for the debt if your daughter is unable to pay.

As for those who argue that introducing their teen to credit-card use is a way of teaching them about financial responsibility, I believe that a far more important financial skill to learn at this age is how to save. Setting a good example of credit-card use is the best thing you can do. If you have too many cards in your wallet and occasionally wake up in the middle of the night wondering how you are ever going to pay them all off, the time has come to rethink your own saving and spending strategies. There are free financial counselling services available in every state that can help you take better control of your finances. The Australian Securities and Investment Commission has a list of them on its website, www.fido.asic.gov.au.

Encourage saving.
If you have not already set up a savings account for your daughter, now is the time. Reveal to her the magic of compound interest: that by keeping her money in her savings account she will earn interest on her accrued interest, that is, she will make money without lifting a finger. And if she puts even a small amount from her allowance or wages into her savings account on a regular basis, the compound interest will pile up even faster.

Learn to say no to nagging.

Companies know that one of the greatest selling tools at their disposal is the nag factor; through ads and other marketing ploys they actively encourage children to nag – the marketers actually refer to this as 'pester power.' You may have been subjected to the onslaught for so many years that a pattern has developed where you refuse, refuse, refuse . . . and eventually give in when it becomes too much to bear. This only reinforces kids' reliance on the nagging strategy.

Each time, weigh up how important this particular product is to your daughter. If you truly believe that this is not something she needs or that you can't afford it, stick to your guns. Alternatives you can offer your daughter include you footing part of the bill while she contributes the rest from her allowance or part-time wages; helping her set up a savings plan so she can work towards affording it herself; or asking her to take on extra chores around the house until she has earned it. If the nagging strategy stops being effective for your teen – that is, you stop giving in to it – she may ease up on the nagging, which no doubt would be a welcome relief to the entire household.

Encourage eclectic shopping.

Next time you go out shopping with your daughter, mix up the mall shopping with a trip to the local Vinnies or Lifeline to search for vintage finds. Hunting for treasures is fun, especially when you snag a really chic item. It's cheap. It's a way for your daughter to put her own individual stamp on her look, an antidote to the dressed-entirely-in-recognisable-labels trend. And the vintage look gets the fashionista nod of approval.

Stand by your own individual style, too. You don't always have to get another's say-so before you buy an item. If your daughter shakes her head when you pick something up, don't immediately put it down. If you really like it and want to wear it, buying it will show your daughter that the sky doesn't cave in when you act without the tribe's approval.

Celebrate giving.

Girls are not born materialistic; it is something they learn as they absorb messages from the culture around them. In fact, the pressure to keep up with everyone else's consumerist expectations can weigh heavily on a girl who doesn't want as many 'things' as other girls do or that adults expect her to. It can come to a head around big gift-giving times such as her birthday and Christmas.

I met a wonderful girl once who had actually been dreading her 14th birthday. There was the persistent question 'What do you want?' to which she drew a blank; and she wasn't looking forward to a big birthday party and opening all the presents (that she felt she didn't need). Sensing her daughter's stress, her mum asked what would *really* make her happy on her birthday. The girl decided that she didn't want her friends to bring her presents; she wanted them to bring presents *for dogs*. On her birthday, she happily tore open the beautifully wrapped dog toys and treats, and then she went with some of her friends to the local dog shelter and gave the dogs all the presents. She and her friends agree that it was their favourite birthday party ever.

This was one smart mother who was sensitive to what

made her daughter tick. A dog birthday party might not be exactly the right thing for your teenage daughter, but as this story shows, you can be creative in your approach to gift giving. By listening to the cues she is sending, you may discover new ways to celebrate the milestones in your daughter's life, and end up giving her memories that will last longer than material gifts.

Appreciate all that money can buy.
I believe that girls have a strong sense of social justice and an urge to be socially responsible and nurturing of others. Just like the girl who wanted to help homeless dogs on her birthday, many girls are just waiting for the opportunity to share, to give. I tell girls that wanting to make money is not bad, because with money you can help to change the world. Sometimes with groups of girls I work with, I demonstrate this by making a donation to World Vision in the girls' names. The money – less than 30 dollars – provides immunisation to protect children in third-world countries from deadly diseases. I see a switch being turned on in these girls' minds when they realise that this relatively small amount of money, given in their own names, will actually save people's lives.

There are plenty of opportunities to get involved in helping others by making donations or doing volunteer work for causes that mean something to you and your daughter. The key is not to lecture or to impose this on your daughter, but to get her input and allow her to have control over whom she helps, and how.

Appreciate all that money cannot buy.

As a much-needed reminder of the things in your life that are more valuable than any price tag can convey, you and your daughter can try this exercise, inspired by a contest in which children were asked to submit a short essay or artwork on the topic 'What I really want that money can't buy'. The kids' answers were compelling, such as the winning essay:

> *What I really want that money can't buy is unconditional love . . . My parents love me and buy me many things. But what tells me they love me the most is when they listen to me. Things are great, but what I really want is their time. What my friends really want is their parents' time. Maybe go for a walk, and talk. Maybe a bike ride and a lecture talk about money. If you just do stuff together and smile, I will know you love me.*
>
> *Erika C, 14*

Try writing down your own answers. You and your daughter may both be surprised by what is revealed.

Affirmations

My own value is greater than any designer label.

I am free to develop my own sense of style.

7

Rage and Despair: Girls in Crisis

❧

Helping adolescent girls in crisis is
about fixing broken connections with them.
It's as deceptively simple as that.

Martha B. Straus, *Adolescent Girls in Crisis*

Abigail was always a challenging baby for her mother, Leigh (not their real names). But it was when she reached Year 9 at school that things truly came to a head. At 14, Abbie was far more unruly and disrespectful of her parents than other girls her age. Struggling to cope with life, angry and unhappy, she had reached crisis point. She tried to take her life by overdosing on paracetamol and was hospitalised. Since then, Leigh says, 'our daughter has continued to slip further and further into a dark hole that we cannot reach her from.'

Abigail left school at the end of Year 10, went to business college and now, aged 18, works in an office. 'It is remarkable that through everything she can keep a good job,' says Leigh. Adept at hiding her pain not only from her co-workers but also from the many doctors Leigh has taken her to, Abbie 'is very good at masking what is really happening in her life and only our family really sees how chaotic things are for her. She is excellent at convincing people she is fine.' But she is far from fine. She thinks she is ugly and worthless, vomits after meals, tells her parents she wants to die and has resorted to cutting herself to deal with her feelings.

Abigail and her family are living through one of the most-feared scenarios of any parent, when their child's passage through adolescence becomes frighteningly dark. As painful as it is for us as mothers to contemplate such darkness in our daughters, we cannot deny that for some girls, adolescence is not just a time of change and growth but one in which serious or life-threatening problems arise.

You are not alone if the mere idea of your daughter wanting to hurt, starve or obliterate herself is hard to bear. The problems for teen girls, the causes and their solutions, are so complex they may seem overwhelming. To bring clarity and to dispel fear, what we need is a safe and supportive place to start from. That's what I hope to provide in this chapter: a starting place so you can find your feet and move on – less anxious, more prepared and more hopeful. I will look at eating disorders, self-harm, depression, suicide and substance abuse. This is by no means an exhaustive list of all the challenges you and your daughter potentially face, but I am hoping it is a helpful cross-section of the crises affecting girls and women.

Leigh has a wish for the future with her daughter that is likely to strike a chord with any mother, whether her daughter is in crisis or not: 'What I'd really like is honesty, and to enjoy spending time with Abbie, and for her to enjoy her life.' I cannot offer a panacea that will magically cure a girl who has anorexia, depression or any other such serious problem. Nor is there a vaccine to prevent your daughter from suffering in the future. But by strengthening your daughter's connections – to you, the rest of the family, her friends, community and school – you can give her the best chance.

Why are girls in crisis?

While each girl's situation at home, school, with friends and in the community influences her life in a unique way, there are underlying factors in our culture that are putting more teenage girls at risk than ever before. Respected therapist and author Martha B. Straus describes it best when she says girls 'are in a crisis of rage and despair'. I believe that understanding and acknowledging this rage and despair are the first steps towards healing this generation of teen girls.

Being part of society means meeting certain expectations; around adolescence girls begin to be more fully aware of the pressure to fulfil these expectations, which were mapped out before they were even born. Girls learn they will be rewarded with praise and acceptance if they fit into an ideal: they should be feminine girls, on the way to becoming feminine women. For teenage girls just beginning to become independent and to master their talents, the feminine ideal can seem frustratingly narrow: pretty, thin, attractive, friendly, agreeable, selfless, nurturing and soft-hearted. There is nothing wrong with these qualities. But a problem arises when adolescent girls feel pressured to act this way to the exclusion of other, more 'masculine' qualities in themselves, such as assertiveness, leadership, courage, physical strength, competitiveness, ambition and clear-headedness. Girls can hardly miss the messages from the people around them, school and popular culture about what it takes to be an ideal girl or woman. Unable to match the ideal no matter how they try, many girls begin to loathe themselves for falling short. Many women continue this self-loathing in their adult lives.

To try to meet the expectations of who they should be, teenage girls may have to tame themselves, blunt themselves. They learn that if they express anger, they will turn people off, because feminine, good girls are agreeable, not cranky. Swallowing anger can lead to confusing teen-girl behaviour. Even though on the surface your daughter may appear sad, happy or indifferent, she may really be bottling up rage. Where does girls' suppressed anger go? For some, it may gradually become depression. Girls may seek escape in drugs and alcohol. And for some, anger transforms into self-aggression: anorexia, bulimia, self-harm, suicide. Similarly, girls tend to be wary of fully displaying their intellect or admitting to other 'bad' emotions such as jealousy, guilt, loneliness, insecurity, sadness and anxiety.

Though adolescence is generally seen as a time of growth and development, there is also an aspect of loss during these years. You may grieve for the time when your daughter was a little girl and feel a certain sadness at how quickly she is growing up. Well, she may also be experiencing her own sense of loss. For your daughter, moving towards adulthood means gaining wonderful things such as more independence, but it also means giving up the much closer bond she had with you when she was little, all the hugging and cuddling she used to get that has inexplicably dried up, and her simpler, prepubescent body that wasn't a source of angst.

Eating disorders

In the eating disorder *anorexia nervosa*, a girl drastically reduces her food intake. In *bulimia nervosa*, she binges, eating excessive amounts of high-calorie foods, then soon after purges the food by vomiting. Feeling guilty and ashamed, she may not eat for several days after a binge. Bulimia tends to be a more hidden condition because a bulimic may be closer to an average weight, while in time an anorexic girl is likely to become visibly starved. One teen who has had bulimia nervosa for eight years told me, 'I'm at a normal weight now and if you saw me on the street, you wouldn't think I had an eating disorder at all.' Girls with anorexia or bulimia may maximise their weight loss by excessively exercising, or taking laxatives, diet pills or diuretics (which are normally used to reduce water retention).

Generally, a girl with anorexia or bulimia has a distorted view of her own body. She is likely to think she is ugly; and even if she is dangerously thin, she may look in the mirror and see herself as very overweight. She may believe she is inherently worthless, a bad girl who deserves to be punished. Her waking hours revolve around food, her weight and her appearance, but she is unaware that her self-perceptions and harsh dietary rules are dysfunctional. Focusing on these things and exerting strict control over her body may be her way of dealing with difficult emotions or a sense of lack of control over other aspects of her life.

An eating disorder that gets less media attention than anorexia and bulimia is binge-eating disorder. A girl with this disorder will eat excessive amounts of food, often in secret, without purging afterwards. Underlying the condition there can be feelings of shame, guilt, self-loathing, depression and difficulty expressing feelings.

All eating disorders exact a terrible toll on a girl's health. Anorexia and bulimia affect all of the body's systems, from the skin, hair, teeth and nails through to all the body's tissues and internal organs, especially the heart and kidneys. Loss of menstrual periods and infertility can occur. In severe cases, death results from heart attack or organ failure. Binge-eating disorder carries with it health risks such as heart disease, stroke and diabetes.

Girls with anorexia or bulimia are often perfectionists and they may see asking for help to combat the disorder as a sign of moral weakness. A teenage girl may cling to her eating disorder in the belief that it is the only way she can cope with the stresses of life. This means that telling a girl with an eating disorder to 'just snap out of it' will only make it seem to her that you don't understand. What she needs is caring help from professionals with experience in adolescent mental health and eating disorders. There can be many facets to treatment. A girl may have regular sessions with a therapist. It may help her if the whole family also has therapy sessions together. Antidepressant or anti-anxiety medication may be prescribed by a specialist, and your GP and a nutritionist may be involved in treatment.

The suicide risk of a person who has an eating disorder is 37 times higher than average and it is not uncommon for sufferers to have other problems such as depression, anxiety, substance abuse, the urge to self-harm or prior sexual abuse. For treatment to be truly successful, all such problems need to be addressed.

Apart from round-the-clock exposure to media and advertising images of extremely thin models and celebrities, another disturbing trend in recent years is the arrival of pro-eating-disorder sites on the internet. Known as 'pro-ana' or 'pro-mia' sites, they are online support groups for people with eating disorders who do not want to be treated. The sites are a way for them to share tips on how to lose more weight and evade treatment, and 'thinspiration' in the form of pictures of emaciated women and girls. The effects of these sites can be devastating. One study showed that 96 per cent of adolescents with eating disorders who viewed pro-eating-disorder sites learned new techniques for losing weight and took longer to recover than those who had not viewed such sites. Another study showed that these sites can also endanger people who do not have eating disorders: when a random sample of female university students were shown a pro-ana site, afterwards they had lower self-esteem, saw themselves as heavier than before, and became more preoccupied with exercise and weight loss.

Yet the biggest risk factor for developing an eating disorder is not exposure to shocking websites or images of dangerously thin celebrities. It is something that girls and women regularly encourage each other to try: frequent and extreme dieting. Girls may compete with their friends to reach the lowest weight. 'We often see groups of girls who will go on diets together and when the other girls later resume normal eating patterns, one or two core girls will stay entrenched in this space,' says Dr Brent Waters, former professor of child and adolescent psychiatry at the University of New South Wales.

The attitude at home is just as important as in the schoolyard. There is no use saying to your daughter, 'You're beautiful the way you are. Come on, eat your dinner,' while at the same time you are on a harsh diet and proudly telling your friends how many kilos you lost this week. How often have you heard a woman say, or in fact said yourself, 'I wish I could get anorexia, just for a couple of weeks'? It's always jokey in tone, but beneath it is a kernel of truth that our daughters cannot fail to grasp.

We cannot completely block out the stream of thin-girl images flooding our daughters' lives. What we do have total control over is the example we set, the role model we provide. And that means being mindful of our words, adopting a healthy, balanced way of eating, and learning to love our own bodies.

Early intervention is key to treating an eating disorder, and this means first recognising that starvation dieting is not a natural part of being a teenage girl. Eating disorders have become so commonplace that there is almost an expectation that a girl will show signs of one at some point. Dr Waters says, 'There is an old viewpoint that adolescence is just a difficult stage, yet the evidence shows quite the opposite:

it need not be. Eating disorders, self-harm – all signify real problems of one sort or another that are driving the behaviour. They are not merely rites of passage.'

My mum said to me, when I was first diagnosed, that I was 'too fat to have an eating disorder' and if I lost weight I wouldn't have a problem. I should point out that this statement was not meant with any malice; my mum simply didn't understand the nature of eating disorders back then . . .

If my mother and I could go through this journey all over again, I'm sure there are many things we would change. The first would be to have my mum believe me when I told her so many years ago that I was sick. I think it's important to understand that no one would truly want to develop an eating disorder, so if your teenager confesses that they're struggling with eating or they think they have an eating disorder, it's probably the truth.

Anon., 19, who has bulimia nervosa

Eating disorder warning signs

- Extreme dieting, such as cutting out entire food groups or skipping meals
- Overeating
- Weight loss or gain
- Obsession with appearance or weight
- Loss of menstrual periods or disrupted menstrual cycle
- Sensitivity to the cold

- Faintness, dizziness, fatigue
- Anxiety, depression, irritability or an increase in mood swings
- Withdrawing from friends and family
- An increased interest in preparing food for other people
- Food rituals such as eating certain foods on certain days
- Wearing baggier clothes
- Exercising to an excessive degree
- Frequent excuses for not eating
- Eating slowly, rearranging food on the plate or using other strategies to eat less, such as eating with a teaspoon
- Eating quickly
- Stockpiling food in her bedroom
- Food disappearing from the pantry
- Frequent trips to the bathroom after meals

Self-harm

Self-harm is when a girl purposely injures herself, usually in secret. There are many different ways that a girl might do this, including cutting, burning, biting or branding her skin; hitting herself or banging her head; pulling her hair out; picking and pulling at her skin; or picking at old sores to open them up again.

In some cases it is a form of risk-tasking and rebelling, or even of being accepted into a peer group. In others, it is a sign of deep psychological distress, a way of coping with painful, overwhelming feelings. If a girl finds it hard to express emotions such as anger, sadness or grief, marking her body in this way may be her desperate attempt at self-expression.

A girl numbed by depression or trauma may self-harm in order to feel something again. It can also be a cry for help. A girl who doesn't know who to ask for help, or how, may be using her injured body to send a message. And as with eating disorders, there are girls who self-harm because they feel that they are not in control of aspects of their life; for them, self-harm is a way of asserting control.

During the act of hurting herself, a girl may feel as though she is releasing pent-up steam, as if opening the valve on a pressure cooker; the act brings a temporary sense of relief. But self-harm also brings with it guilt, depression, self-loathing, anger, fear, and isolation from friends and family.

Self-harm doesn't necessarily mean that a girl is suicidal, but all cases of self-harm need to be taken seriously. Self-harm can be related to mental health issues including depression, psychosis, bipolar disorder and borderline personality disorder; to a trauma such as physical or sexual abuse; or to some other source of deep psychological pain. Self-harm may also do lasting physical damage. While girls rarely need hospitalisation because of self-harm, they may give themselves lifelong scarring as well as nerve damage.

In the short term, if your daughter self-harms she needs to learn ways to cope when the urge strikes. Her therapist is likely to suggest ideas such as counting to ten or waiting 15 minutes, to give the feeling a chance to pass; saying 'No!' or 'Stop!'; relaxation techniques such as yoga; or going for a run or doing some other kind of hard physical exercise. But don't be alarmed if some of the advice your daughter receives sounds a little unorthodox: if the urge to self-harm is unbearable to resist, an accepted short-term solution is to choose an alternative, such as squeezing ice cubes between her fingers until they go numb, eating a chilli, standing under a cold shower, having her legs waxed or drawing in red on her body instead of cutting. Crucially, the underlying reasons why she self-harms need to be uncovered and worked through with a professional, who will also help her to develop healthier ways of identifying, coping with and expressing painful emotions.

Self-harm warning signs

- Cuts – especially small shallow parallel cuts on the arms or legs – for which there is no adequate explanation
- Other frequent and unexplained injuries, such as burns or bruises
- Starting to wear long sleeves or pants all the time, even in warm weather
- Sudden aversion to going swimming or getting changed in front of other girls
- Hair missing, where it has been deliberately pulled out
- Mood changes, depression, anxiety
- Spending a lot of time alone
- Notable difficulty dealing with stressful or emotional situations
- A drop in school performance

Depression

Right now, between 2 and 5 per cent of young Australians are suffering from depression. By the time they are adults, around one in five of them will have experienced it. Unfortunately, some of these young people will go through adolescence without their depression being recognised or treated. As we tend to expect that the teenage years will be a turbulent time of extreme emotions, sometimes teen depression slips under the radar.

Depression is not the same as having a blue day now and then, feeling a bit down sometimes or being sad for a brief time in response to a disappointment or loss. These things are a normal part of life for an adolescent – or adult. Depression is a clinical condition involving a disturbance in brain chemistry that causes a change in mood: from a state of equilibrium to one of sadness or irritability. Depression decreases the brain's ability to feel joy and pleasure. For instance, a depressed teen may suddenly stop playing netball or going shopping with her friends. The chemical changes in the brain also affect other body systems and behaviour: a depressed girl's appetite may increase or decrease; she may sleep more or less than usual; she may find it hard to concentrate; and she may feel tired and lacking in energy.

The causes of depression are multilayered and differ from one individual to another. A teen can inherit a predisposition to develop depression. It can be triggered by a stressful event such as the death of a loved one or the divorce of her parents. And personality may play a role, with anxious, self-critical and sensitive people being at greater risk, according to the Black Dog Institute.

It can be tricky to identify depression in teens because they may have real difficulty identifying and explaining how they are feeling. Teens are undergoing so many other developmental changes at the same time that we may also be uncertain whether the changes in their mood and behaviour are simply a normal part of growing up. And rather than a sad mood, the only indication that a teen has depression may be that she starts behaving differently. For instance, she might start to do worse in school, want to spend more time alone, or start doing new risky things such as driving recklessly, being promiscuous, taking drugs or drinking alcohol. You know your daughter best, so trust your gut instincts. If you feel that for a period of two weeks or more she has not been the girl you recognise, seek medical advice.

It is important to treat teen depression as these are important years when a girl undergoes changes that will be crucial to her happiness later in life, such as becoming independent, developing her learning skills, forming her own sexual identity, creating relationships and preparing for her future career. Having depression can interfere with all of these important developments. It also places a girl at greater risk of substance abuse, self-harm and eating disorders. At its most severe, depression can cause a girl to try to take her life.

If you need to seek treatment for your daughter, be prepared to think beyond quick fixes. Your GP is a good starting place, but ask for a referral to someone who specialises in depression or your local adolescent mental health team, rather than have the GP prescribe medication. That is the advice of child and adolescent psychiatrist Dr Brent Waters, who believes that antidepressants are overprescribed for teenagers. Another problem with prescribing antidepressants to teens is that they tend to resist taking any form of medication. 'It is an issue of control,' says Dr Waters. If a teen feels that a doctor is talking down to her or ordering her to take medication, it can make her feel powerless, just at the time when she is 'trying to gain power and freedom, not lose it'.

If antidepressants do become part of your daughter's treatment plan, there are some useful things to know. The specialist is likely to start her on a low dose and raise the dosage gradually over a week or two, and it can be up to eight weeks before the drug begins to have its full effect. Not all antidepressants work on all patients in exactly the same way, so the specialist may recommend swapping to a different type of medication or making further changes to the dosage. With many antidepressants, if a patient suddenly takes herself off the drug – goes 'cold turkey' – it can result in some frightening side effects such as anxiety, insomnia, nausea, and pins and needles. It is vital to follow the instructions when taking an antidepressant and to consult the specialist before coming off it. It is also important that the specialist knows what else your daughter is taking. For instance, taking certain antidepressants with the herbal supplement St John's Wort can result in a dangerous interaction.

Even if it is recommended for your daughter to take antidepressants, psychological treatment will also be important. There are numerous psychological approaches that can help, depending on your daughter's needs. An increasingly common and successful type is cognitive behaviour therapy (CBT), which can be done one-on-one with a therapist or in a small group. The aim of CBT is to reveal the ways in which thought patterns affect mood, and to teach the patient how to challenge their negative thoughts and beliefs. Other types of counselling or therapy may focus on aspects of her personality or events in the past that may have predisposed your daughter to depression.

Depression warning signs

- Uncharacteristic risk-taking such as driving recklessly, being promiscuous, taking drugs or drinking alcohol
- Sadness
- Irritability
- Mood that varies throughout the day, especially feeling worse in the morning and better as the day progresses
- Less interest in doing things she used to enjoy
- Increase or decrease in appetite
- Sleeping more or less than usual
- Restlessness
- Tiredness, fatigue
- A drop in school performance, due to decreased concentration
- Wanting to spend more time alone
- Expressing feelings of guilt, worthlessness or hopelessness
- Increase in sensitivity to pain; new aches and pains
- Apathy; lack of motivation
- Dwelling on death or suicide

Suicide

It may come as a surprise that in females, the highest-risk time for suicide is not the teenage years. The highest rate of suicide in females occurs in the age group that many teen girls' mums belong to: women aged between 35 and 44. In fact, teen girls have the lowest rate of suicide of all females. That statistic is little comfort, of course. Just one teen suicide is too many. Just one adult suicide is too many. The reason that knowing the statistics is helpful is that they remind us to be mindful of not only our teen daughters' emotional health but also our own.

What many people who try to take their lives share is a sense of being trapped in a stressful or painful situation, a situation that they are powerless to change. Having depression or a mental illness raises a person's risk of suicide. Stressful life events or ongoing stressful situations may fuel feelings of desperation or depression that can lead to suicide attempts. Examples of these stresses include the death of a loved one, divorce or a relationship breakup, a child custody dispute, settling in to a blended family, financial trouble, or a serious illness or accident. Any kind of abuse – physical, verbal or sexual – increases the risk, and that applies not only to teens but their mothers and fathers as well, even if that abuse took place many years ago. Substance abuse by any member of a family affects the other members of the family and can lead to suicidal feelings either directly or indirectly, through the loss of income and social networks or trouble with the law.

Looking at teens in particular, bullying needs to be taken seriously as it has been known to make children try to take their own life. Also, teens are right in the middle of forming their own individual identities and a major component of that is their sexuality. For a teenager who is questioning their sexual preference or gender, the pressure to be like everyone else, the taunting they receive because they clearly are not, or their own guilt and confusion can become unbearable. A relationship breakup can be a trigger for suicide in some teens. As adults, we have the ability to look at the bigger picture and know that in years to come, a teenage breakup will not seem anywhere near as important as it does at the time. Your teenage daughter, on the other hand, may not yet have the maturity to see beyond the immediate pain. If she seems unduly distressed about a breakup, pay attention. Another trigger for teen suicide is the recent suicide of someone close to them, or the anniversary of a suicide or death of someone close to them, so these are times when your daughter may need extra support.

Suicide is hard to talk about. It is almost taboo, simply too painful to touch on. But silence can be deadly. Often the parents of a teen girl at risk of suicide do not ask their daughter the tough question of whether she is planning to take her own life. In part they may be in a state of denial, which is only human – after all, no parent wants to imagine that their daughter feels suicidal. They may also have a fear that seems to be ingrained in our culture: that if they mention suicide to their depressed or distressed daughter, they will be putting the idea in her head. But experts in adolescent mental health agree that it is more than okay to speak directly to your daughter about suicide. 'Parents are often worried that by asking they may make matters worse. Well, I have never known a child to suicide because someone asked whether they were thinking about it,' says Dr Brent Waters. 'They should ask; the issues won't just go away.'

Another unhelpful myth about suicide is that a teen who talks about suicide is simply seeking attention and won't actually take her life. In fact, four out of five young people who commit suicide tell someone of their intentions beforehand. Besides, I have never understood the point of making a distinction between attention seeking, a cry for help or a genuine intention to commit suicide. Even if a teen is not actually going to go through with a plan to take her life, if she is distressed enough to cry out for help, her voice needs to be heard and she needs our support.

Suicide warning signs

- Loss of interest in activities she used to enjoy
- Giving away her prized possessions
- Thoroughly cleaning her room and throwing out important things
- Violent or rebellious behaviour
- Running away from home
- Substance abuse
- Taking no interest in her clothes or appearance
- A sudden, marked personality change
- Withdrawal from friends, family and her usual activities
- A seeming increase in her accident proneness, or signs of self-harm
- A change in eating and sleeping patterns
- A drop in school performance, due to decreased concentration and feelings of boredom
- Frequent complaints about stomach aches, headaches, tiredness and other symptoms that may be linked to

emotional upsets
- Rejection of praise or rewards
- Verbal hints such as 'I won't be a problem for you much longer' or 'Nothing matters anyway'
- Suddenly becoming cheerful after a period of being down, which may indicate she has made a resolution to take her life

What you can do

Reading the list of suicide warning signs is enough to chill anyone, but there is much you can do to help someone who is suicidal. Number one: if anyone – child, adolescent or adult – says something like 'I want to kill myself' or 'I'm going to kill myself', seek help straightaway. Remove anything they might be tempted to use to kill themselves with and stay with them. Dial 000 if you need to, or call a crisis line. The following phone counselling services are available throughout Australia 24 hours a day:

- Lifeline: 13 11 14
- Kids Help Line: 1800 55 1800
- Salvation Army 24-hour Care Line: 1300 36 36 22

Another valuable thing you can do to help someone you fear is having suicidal thoughts is to listen. These pointers are adapted from the Victorian Government's excellent 'Youth suicide prevention – the warning signs' on www.betterhealth.vic.gov.au:

- Listen and encourage her to talk
- Tell her you care
- Acknowledge her feelings
- Reassure her
- Gently point out the consequences of her suicide, for her and the people she leaves behind
- Stay calm; try not to panic or get angry
- Try not to interrupt her
- Try not to judge her
- Don't overwhelm her with too much advice or stories about your own experiences

Substance abuse

The greatest fear of many of the parents I meet through Enlighten is that their teenage daughter will be exposed to drugs. I think the reason we as parents are so concerned about drugs is the sheer number of different drugs now, their wider availability and the high toxicity and unpredictability of some of the newer drugs. When we were teenagers, there were a handful of drugs. Now there's also ecstasy, ice, GHB. There is drink-spiking. Date-rape drugs. Pills and powders manufactured in illicit laboratories so people cannot even be certain what they are taking. There is chroming: getting high by inhaling spray-paint fumes. There is the inhalation of petrol, glue and solvents. Potentially lethal painkillers and sedatives are sold through chemists, such as the ones that took the life of Heath Ledger in 2008. And there is poly-drug use, when a person takes a cocktail of legal and/or illicit drugs, leading to an increased and more unpredictable risk of overdose and dangerous side effects. It's no wonder we feel a little panicky sometimes.

Panic can be a paralysing thing. Knowledge, however, is empowering. Our greatest fears often focus on harder drugs such as heroin, cocaine, ecstasy and crystal meth (ice), but these are in fact the drugs that teens are least likely to be exposed to. Heroin, cocaine and ecstasy are used by fewer than three teenagers in every hundred. Amphetamines such as speed and crystal meth are used by four in every hundred. On the other hand, 25 in every hundred teens have gotten high by inhaling spray paint, petrol, glue or solvent fumes. These are readily available and the practice is damaging to vital organs, including the brain. That their teen will die from overdosing on hard drugs is one of most parents' greatest fears. Death from substance abuse at any age is tragic, but when a person dies so young, they lose so many years of life. And the emotional cost to their family and friends is immeasurable. But to put the risk in perspective, drugs account for 6 per cent of deaths each year in people aged 15 to 24.

Hard drugs indeed devastate or end the lives of the teens who use them, so we need to do everything in our power to stop their use. Yet in our concern about hard drugs, it is important that we don't lose sight of the less headline-grabbing substances that larger numbers of teens are abusing. It turns out that two of the substances teens widely abuse are also the most widely abused by adults: alcohol and tobacco. The other is one that plenty of adults have used and that some even mistakenly believe is quite benign: marijuana. Perhaps the reason teen abuse of alcohol, tobacco and marijuana doesn't cause as much alarm is that so many adults have also used or are currently using them.

The statistics also show that efforts to curb teen substance abuse seem to pay off. From 2004 to 2007, the number of teen boys using illicit drugs dropped from 20 to 15 per cent. In 2007, 18 per cent of girls used illicit drugs, a drop of 4 per cent. The number of all teens who smoked cigarettes fell; in the 16–17 year age group, the number fell by about half.

I offer these statistics to provide some context, not to diminish the toll drugs take on the kids who use them. Serious health risks go hand-in-hand with drug abuse. Depending on the drug and how heavy a person's use is, substance abuse can cause damage to the heart, kidneys, liver and brain; blood-borne diseases such as hepatitis B and C, and HIV; accidents; psychosis; depression; and coma or death. Not only can some drugs contribute to brain damage, they can in fact change the way the brain works. This is of special concern for teenagers, because the different parts of their brains are developing at different rates. In teens, the part of the brain that is geared towards avoiding risks is under-developed in relation to the reward or pleasure centre of the brain.

'We know that adolescent brains are driven by reward, and younger people often do not have the brain maturity to put the brakes on things,' says Associate Professor Michael Baigent, senior consultant psychiatrist at Flinders Medical Centre.

This brain difference, teens' strong urge to fit in with friends and the stresses that sometimes come with adolescence make teens more vulnerable to substance abuse. But in our concern for our daughters' safety, we should avoid pre-judging or making assumptions about teens, painting them all with the same brush. 'Society can create a certain amount of distrust of young people,' clinical psychologist Clive Skene says. He urges us to connect with our teens as individuals: 'We have to be careful because every human being is capable of being influenced positively and negatively.'

If most drugs are taken regularly enough, a person's tolerance increases and so they need increasing dosages to get an effect. As they become more dependent, without the drug they suffer withdrawal symptoms. Often a drug problem is one problem among others such as depression or an eating disorder, and in order to help someone kick their dependence, these need to be treated as well. Treatment may have several aspects, depending on the type of substance abuse and the individual. Counselling, family therapy, CBT and group meetings such as Alcoholics Anonymous or Narcotics Anonymous are some of the current treatments. Medication sometimes is prescribed, as treatment for other conditions such as depression or anxiety, or for easing withdrawal symptoms, suppressing drug cravings or blocking the effects of a drug so it becomes pointless to take it. In the first instance, for help with a teen's drug addiction talk to your GP or community health centre for referral to a counsellor with experience in substance abuse.

Substance abuse warning signs

- Mood swings
- Depression
- Confusion

- Agitation and irritability
- Missing school or skipping classes
- A drop in school performance
- Getting into fights
- Starting arguments with you or breaking rules more often
- Changes in taste in music, hair or clothing, to a more unconventional style
- Withdrawal from the family
- Hanging out with a new, possibly older, crowd
- A significant weight gain or loss
- Red or glassy eyes
- Extreme fatigue
- Poor health

Prevention and intervention

I believe that there is much we can do to help prevent our daughters finding themselves at crisis point, and that no matter how troubled a girl is, she can turn her life around. The key is communication, and 'mothers and daughters have a natural advantage in that they seem to both be naturally built for dialogue,' says child and adolescent psychiatrist Dr Brent Waters. 'It's a little like parenting toddlers: as long as they were making noise, we knew what they were up to and we could step in if we needed to, to keep them safe. It was only when they were quiet that we knew it was time to get alarmed! Having teenagers is really no different. Don't ask them to account for every second of their day, don't over-parent, yet don't stop talking and listening, either.'

Girls regularly tell me that what they want more of is their parents' time. They want their parents to listen. Sometimes when we ask our daughters what's wrong, we get a blank gaze or a huff or a slammed door, and we give up. Don't give up too quickly. Your girl may be sending out all the signals to push you away while actually she needs you to keep asking, giving her attention, showing her you care. Therapist Martha B. Straus urges: 'When she's at a loss for words, guess and guess again.' Many teens have a limited vocabulary for expressing their feelings, but we can help. It can take something as simple as 'I feel really angry about this – do you?' to open the floodgates. The questions set out in Appendix 3, 'Let's Talk', are good conversation starters.

One of the most helpful things you can do is allow her to express all her emotions, rather than choking on her darker feelings until they turn into despair. 'When girls can be angry,' Straus writes, 'they can also be reassured they are worth such powerful feelings – there is someone in there worth being mad about.'

Action Plan
Seek professional help.
If you feel that your daughter is showing warning signs of risky behaviour or a mood disorder, a good starting point is your GP, for a referral to a relevant specialist, local adolescent mental health team, counsellor or community health centre. Medicare rebates are available for referrals to psychiatrists, clinical psychologists and social workers. For older teens especially, it may be easier said than done to seek

professional help. If your daughter does not accept treatment, try to keep the lines of communication open; let her know that you are there to offer support and help her get treatment if she changes her mind. Professional advice will be valuable for you and the rest of your family, even if your daughter refuses help for herself. A professional can provide much-needed support for you as well as guide you in how to best manage your daughter's situation.

Be consistent.

With any teen, and especially a teen who takes risks or self-harms, it is essential to set consistent boundaries, so she knows what behaviour is expected of her. Try to maintain a united front with your partner or other adult caregivers, because if you seem divided, she may try to capitalise on that. Try to be consistent in your loving, as well. Even if your daughter takes a drastic backslide in her recovery, she needs to know that you still love her and are willing to try again with her.

Banish secrecy.

When a family member is in the midst of a crisis, a common reflex is to try to keep it secret from the outside world. Attempted suicide, an eating disorder, financial problems – whatever the crisis is, the tendency is to try and contain it within our own four walls, out of embarrassment or an instinct to protect our family from judgement, pity or bullying. Maintaining a shroud of secrecy around a crisis is not helpful to our children, though. This is particularly so with girls, 'as secrets can be a dark thing within teen girl networks and a source of power for the holder of the secret,' according to Dr Waters. 'Parents need to reframe the issue: it is not to be a "secret", rather it may be "private".'

Build networks of support for your daughter.

For teen girls, life is all about networks. The best way to prevent problems, or support your daughter on the road to recovery, is help her forge strong, healthy networks. Her networks may include doctors, therapists, adult mentors, other relatives, school counsellors, and friends at school and out of school.

Find a confidante.

Leigh, mother of 18-year-old Abigail, who self-harms and has an eating disorder, suggests that mothers in similar situations find a 'safe person', a non-judgemental friend to talk to if the going gets tough. She and her husband each have their own separate safe person they can offload to in confidence. Remember, too, that if you need help from any of your friends or adult family members, it is okay to ask.

Give a Book of Love.

This is an idea that I was told about by a teen with an eating disorder. When I asked her to tell me the most healing thing someone had done for her, she said that it was when a friend sent her a Book of Love. 'It was just before I went into the most intensive treatment I've ever been in and I received a package in the mail,' she recalls. 'She'd filled a book with song lyrics, things she likes about me, inspiring quotes, and pretty stickers and other glittery things . . . She hadn't told me she was going to send it, and it was such a lovely surprise. She left the last ten pages blank for me to fill in with positive things about myself.' As with many people who have an eating disorder, this girl is also dealing with other issues: depression, anxiety, and a past history of suicide attempts and self-harm. I think the Book of Love is relevant for girls dealing with all such issues, to remind them how much they are cherished.

Organise respite care.

If your daughter has an ongoing serious problem, you may be so busy supporting her that you don't look after yourself. You need a chance to recharge your batteries, eat well, exercise, and connect with your friends, family or partner. Official respite care services for parents are hard to find, so this is when you probably need to call upon friends and family to spend time with your daughter so that you can have a break. It could be as simple as getting out to a yoga class once a week. If this feels selfish to you, remember that we all at our strongest and most supportive when we're refreshed, healthy and manage our stress.

Celebrate.

When your daughter is on the path to recovery there may be frustrating and disappointing setbacks, but there will be victories, too. Take heart in them. And celebrate.

Affirmations

I listen with love, respect and an open heart.

I ask for help when I need it.

8

Schooling for Life

So much has changed since I was at school, I wouldn't
know where to start in helping my daughter out! I mean,
when I was at school we wrote down the teacher's
notes from the blackboard most of the day. My daughter
comes home telling me about PowerPoint presentations,
podcasts . . . Rather than the classics, they study films
and the lyrics to songs I have never even heard of . . . I
feel completely out of my depth so I just stay out of it.

Christine, the mother of a 14-year-old girl

Once girls reach high school, parents can feel ill equipped
to help them learn. The 'really big school' can seem
impersonal and overwhelming. The curriculum is more complex. There are new school subjects today that we couldn't
have even imagined when we were at school. Some of the
information our teens are learning is outside our realm of
experience. Yet teenagers spend only 15 per cent of their time
at school, which means our support at home is still essential.

Helping your daughter get the most out of her schooling
is not as overwhelming as it may seem. The most important

thing girls are acquiring at school today is no different to the most important thing we acquired at school: *learning skills*. Regardless of how curriculums change or technology advances, at the core of a successful high school education is the development of lifelong learning skills. These learning skills are what have helped us in our tertiary studies, careers and adult life in general. The same will be true for our daughters. What really matters is not the fact that your girl is learning by listening to a podcast rather than by writing down notes off a blackboard; it's the fundamental skills she's developing for the future, such as the ability to learn new things, how to communicate with others and work in a team, planning and organisation, problem-solving, self-management and initiative.

It is especially important for our teen daughters to master these core skills because the world is rapidly changing. It is impossible for the educators who set high school curriculums to know for certain what students will need to know in the future. Even seemingly modern teaching techniques such as the use of podcasts will seem quaint in a few years' time. Schools are realising that they need to keep pace with change. They are focusing on helping students become lifelong learners who can adapt to changes in the world and in the workplace. Greg Whitby, who is the Executive Director of Catholic Schools for Western Sydney, writes:

> [T]hose who work in and for schools will have to work differently if they are to serve their students and society in the knowledge age of the 21st century . . . We stand together at the beginning of a transformation of schooling for life.

When I was a high school teacher, one of my biggest frustrations at parent-teacher evenings was trying to convey everything I needed to in the five minutes that were allocated for each meeting. Here I can take the time to share the words of wisdom I have gathered during my years of teaching – and learning – in schools. The advice offered here is tailored towards mothers helping their daughters reach their full potential but is equally relevant for dads; and much of it can be applied to help teen boys, too.

Learning like a girl

If we are going to help our daughters to learn, we need to know what learning styles and techniques work best for them. Learning styles tend to differ between girls and boys. This may partly be due to the difference in the ways that girls and boys are nurtured, but there are also differences in brain development and cognitive (thinking) development between boys and girls. According to the experts – and my years of experience in classrooms back this up – girls tend to have better language skills than boys of the same age. Girls usually talk more, have a wider vocabulary, and are more comfortable discussing and writing about their emotions. Connections are important to teen girls in every part of life, including education: they are more interested in studying with their peers. Girls are also able to concentrate for longer periods than boys. While boys often take an interest in technical details and processes, girls tend to be more engaged when they can see a practical application and usefulness to what they're learning. It may not be maths, science and computing that many girls struggle with, but rather the way in which they are taught: if real-world examples are given and girls have the opportunity to apply their new knowledge, they may be better able to connect with those subjects.

These are general guidelines that may help you understand broadly how your daughter learns. With these as a foundation, you can encourage more opportunities for her to learn in ways that work for her – group study, discussion groups, practical application of knowledge – and minimise attitudes that are less helpful, such as expecting her to study alone all the time or to memorise technical details without context.

There are exceptions to every rule, though. Each individual, whether girl or boy, is unique. People are influenced by more than just their gender, so you do need to be mindful that your daughter may differ in some respects from other girls. These differences can be beneficial: for instance, a girl might be switched on by learning about processes in a theoretical way as well as having better language skills than boys her age. Differences can also be frustrating: think of a girl whose language skills are not quite as developed as those of the other girls in her year at school, when there is an assumption that English should come relatively easy to her. The better we understand a child's individual learning preferences, the better we can support them and get them additional help if they need it.

Get to know your daughter's studying habits and ask yourself: how does she like to learn? When, how and with whom does she do her best learning? If you are unsure, ask her and ask her teachers. Find out what works and how you can make her learning environment at home even better. For more specific guidance on how to do this, I think Elizabeth Hartley-Brewer, a respected parenting author, has a helpful way of looking at the role of a parent in a child's education. She likens it to the role a good sports coach has in an athlete's training:

> From sports psychology, we know the best coaches focus on improving technique and skill . . . They make rewards reflect achievements; teach individuals to manage their own mistakes, learning and progress; and reduce anxiety by finding out what is causing it and addressing that directly.

Rather than being overwhelmed by how to help your daughter learn school subjects you don't entirely understand, you can use the idea of becoming her coach to break down your role into doable tasks: helping your daughter improve her techniques and skills; rewarding her achievements; allowing her to learn from her mistakes; giving her the freedom to manage her own learning; and offering her your loving support, so that she is not left feeling anxious.

Improving techniques and skills

The three R's – reading, 'riting and 'rithmetic – were once considered the basics of learning. But new technology means that the three R's are now just a few of the tools a girl needs in her backpack. To make use of all the learning opportunities that will come her way in the future, a teen girl also needs to be competent in a wide range of information and communications technology (ICT). Yet while girls are, on average, more successful at reading and writing than boys, evidence shows that girls are in trouble when it comes to ICT literacy. They are just not embracing the cyber world to the same degree as boys.

In Australia, girls are more likely than boys to see ICT as boring (36 per cent of girls compared to 16 per cent of boys) or difficult (23 per cent to 11 per cent). The result is that more boys than girls study technology-related subjects. Out of all the students who took computer programming in the 2002 Higher School Certificate in New South Wales, less than one in five were female. The same trend was seen in TAFE enrolments. Girls and young women are at risk of becoming the information-poor and of being excluded from emerging technology jobs and fields of study.

To help address this imbalance, we should coach our girls to play to their strengths. 'Rather than trying to find ways to help girls use computers in the same ways boys do,' writes educator Bronwyn T. Williams, we need to ask ourselves: '[H]ow do we help them build on their strengths to find new, creative, and feminist ways of designing and using computers?' If girls are less interested than boys in learning computer programming and software design, perhaps it is because they don't consider this knowledge relevant to them. Girls tend to like connecting and communicating, and learn best when they can see the practical application of knowledge. Well, computer literacy is crucial to creating the kind of websites that offer girls a chance to communicate and connect, such as MySpace and Facebook, blogs and role-playing sites. Encouraging girls to see this link and to become involved can bring computing subjects to life for them. Another reason girls may lack interest in computing is that there are few positive female role models for girls within ICT; if possible, finding a female mentor for your daughter may be beneficial.

Highlighting the practical application of knowledge is the learning 'on' switch for so many girls that it can be used to help them develop skills in any field, not just ICT. This was brought home to me when I was running The Lighthouse Project, a mentoring program for young people at risk of leaving school early. One of the volunteer mentors, a dedicated man named Glenn, was an officer in the RAAF. He was mentoring Rachel, a 14-year-old girl who found school irrelevant and boring, and had developed a sense of despair about her schooling.

Even though she didn't like science and maths at school, Glenn got her working in a highly technical arena where there could be no margin of error: a division known as 'Air Movements' at the RAAF base in Richmond, New South Wales. This is the team that calculates safe loads for aircraft used in airlifts, such as the C-130, B707 and Caribou.

'Later, when we debriefed, Rachel recalled how boring it was poring over numbers, shapes, weights and dangerous cargo types,' says Glenn. Yet he couldn't help but notice that she was very taken with a good-looking pilot she had met. 'Then it dawned on me,' he says. 'I asked Rachel what all the science and maths she was continually complaining about, and couldn't understand, was useful for. The normal "Nothing" reply followed. I explained that the good-looking pilot's life was partly in her hands. I explained that the aircraft was like a seesaw. It needed to be perfectly balanced.' To avoid dangerous chemical reactions, he explained to Rachel, some types of cargo needed to be separated from others, by varying distances.

'And if it wasn't, I told her, the good-looking pilot's flight would be his last, and it would be the last of everybody else on board . . . To watch Rachel's face was like watching fireworks light up the night sky . . . She immediately grabbed the tables we use to calculate the necessary ratios and began asking intelligent, urgent questions so that she could help figure out the equations we needed to get the weight and balance ratio correct.'

Glenn was observant enough to find what it was that would turn the key so that Rachel, once unlikely to finish school, let alone be into science and maths, was suddenly passionately interested. For each girl there is something that will make learning relevant. Our role is to keep the lines of communication with our daughters open so we can discover what it is that makes them want to learn, and then to capitalise on that at every opportunity.

Rewarding achievement

One of the stubborn stereotypes about girls is that they lack the competitive spirit seen in boys. Too many people still believe that it is only boys, fuelled by testosterone and bravado, who are motivated by competition, who strive because they want to be victorious on the sporting field or in the classroom. This is absolute nonsense. Certainly I

was a very competitive girl. At school, I wanted to be top
of the class. At my part-time job at McDonalds, I thrived
on being the fastest girl on the register. Even socially, I
wanted to have as many friends as I could. What drove me
were the emotional rewards: I would be noticed; I would
be valued.

Though the competitive urge of girls is often underestimated, it can be a powerful tool for helping them learn.

What this means for you at home is getting to know which
rewards motivate your daughter the most. To be meaningful,
the reward needs to be relative to the achievement – neither
too outlandish nor too meagre – and needs to be something
she will appreciate.

Managing mistakes

We are in the midst of an overprotective parenting trend
known as 'cotton-wool' or 'parachute' parenting, in which
adults try to protect children from every conceivable danger
and conflict. This ranges from banning kids from walking
anywhere in case they are bullied, hit by a car or targeted
by a paedophile, through to parents intervening in even the
most minor problems their children have at school or with
friends.

The urge to protect our children is a natural one. But
this instinct has been transformed by an armoury of technology that allows parents and children to check in with
one another 24/7. We want to monitor our kids more often
because, with continuous media exposure, we are all too
aware of the accidents and crimes that can happen. And

on average, we are having fewer children, later in life, and more often with the help of fertility treatments. Children have always been – and should always be – precious to their parents. It's just that never before have there seemed to be so many reasons to protect kids; nor have there ever been so many ways to monitor them.

Even though our intentions are good, when we overprotect teens we are actually taking away a much-needed learning opportunity: the opportunity to learn from their mistakes. The result of too much adult intervention is that a teen may have difficulty perceiving real danger, solving problems and resolving conflicts with others. Consultant psychologist Dr Judith Paphazy, who has worked with students, teachers and parents in Australian schools, believes that 'children are becoming less resilient and self-reliant' because of cotton-wool parenting. Self-reliance is essential so teens can go on to make wise independent choices as adults; resilience will allow them to cope with the disappointments and failures that every person must face in life.

Fear of failure can be paralysing. 'A lot of girls I have had contact with are frightened into inaction,' says Lisa Porter, Acting Head of Student Welfare at Sydney's Fairfield High School. 'They have so many worries about the future that it is as though they are playing a game of chess and rather than risk a pawn, they don't play at all.' A prime example of this is when the time comes for girls to make subject choices. 'They are afraid of making a "wrong" decision, so they take the courses their friends are doing or that their parents recommend, rather than going out on a limb and choosing something they enjoy or would like to try.'

Teen girls need our reassurance that it's okay to take *informed risks* with their education. Just as they need to learn to take informed risks in their lives in general. You will not be there to help your daughter make decisions as an adult, and nor should you be. Your daughter needs to learn problem-solving and decision-making skills now if she is to be a self-reliant, resilient, well-balanced adult. Your daughter will make some mistakes along the way. It may be hard to resist stepping in to solve all her problems. But your job now is to be there for support and comfort and to offer advice if she asks for it. And when she does trip up, try not to say 'I told you so.' (Even if you did!)

The worst thing about being a teen girl is people condemning you when you fall when, in fact, you only just tripped and learned something.

Yan, 16

A mother should share personal failures as well as successes and explain to her daughter what she may have learnt from mistakes. It gives daughters hope that they too can move on after a poor choice.

Amelia Toffoli, Principal, St Brigid's Girls School, WA

'Don't fear mistakes; they're an investment in learning.'

Elizabeth Broderick, Sex Discrimination
Commissioner and Commissioner
responsible for Age Discrimination

Managing learning

As coach, one of our goals is to help our daughter manage her own learning. For most of us, the greatest test of our patience in this regard comes at homework time. Girls tell me that many of the arguments they have with their parents are about homework. (That, and the state of their bedrooms!)

I am not a big fan of students having to do lots of homework, particularly in the primary and early high school years. Homework can be highly valuable and stimulating, such as a project where the student is allowed to choose her own topic and explore it in her own way. But I think students are often given homework that is less rewarding than that, because teachers feel pressure to set 'busy work'. This pressure may come from parents who believe that lots of homework means lots of learning. It concerns me that by setting too much homework we may in fact be creating bad work habits by sending a message to students that if tasks are not completed during class time they can be completed at home. If as adults we managed our time more effectively, perhaps we would not need to take piles of work home to complete, either.

Regardless of my reservations about the type and amount of homework teens have, the reality is that the situation is unlikely to change any time soon. In the first few years of high school, students are usually set up to one hour per night of homework, increasing to three and a half hours per night by the end of high school.

There are some parents who think they are helping their teenage daughter cope with her workload by completing her homework or polishing her assignments for her. No good can come from this. The girl whose parents become this involved may receive good marks for her assignments but will learn nothing – except that she is not smart enough in her parents' eyes and that her best efforts will never be good enough. What we *can* do to help our daughters is try to promote a positive attitude about homework and studying, a good environment for doing it in and effective time-management strategies.

The traditional idea of a good studying environment is something akin to a cloister: unless a student is in seclusion, in total silence, bent over her books like a monastic scribe for hours on end, she isn't really studying. But you *can* allow your daughter some wiggle room here. There are a variety of learning environments, each of which is valid at the right time.

Sometimes, girls (and boys) benefit from learning in a collaborative, interactive way. When a girl is required to sit alone at her desk in her room for hours, she may feel banished and view her isolation as a punishment, which will hardly encourage her to find joy in learning. Many girls I speak to tell me they would prefer to be allowed to be social learners, working with their friends. Indeed, the *understanding* phase of learning can be genuinely enhanced when girls are encouraged to work together outside school. Good examples are when students are brainstorming before they commence writing an essay, or when they are producing summaries of a topic, which they will use later when revising. Of course, there are times when private work is essential to completing a task. For example, writing an essay is not a group task.

Studying with a group of friends may provide an

environment that is less threatening than the classroom, where a girl may hesitate to express her opinion or may not receive as much encouragement to. With her study friends, a girl has more opportunity to express her views and question others and develop new ways of thinking. Yes, there will be some off-task chitchat, but that's okay, so long as the girls are encouraged to be responsible and set clear goals at the outset of their study group meeting. For example, they might agree that by 4.30 pm they are to have identified and discussed the three main themes in the film *Rabbit-proof Fence*, or whatever it is they are currently studying in class.

Allowing your daughter to work with friends when appropriate gives her the freedom to make her own decisions and to manage her own learning. Not only does it give her the chance to learn about the actual topics the girls are studying, it also encourages her to develop planning, organisation and time-management skills, the ability to collect and analyse information, and teamwork and communication skills. Importantly, she will also begin recognising which tasks are best done in isolation and which ones are enhanced by discussion with others. The time she does spend studying solo will begin to feel less like a punishment and more like her own smart work choice.

> One time all my friends went to a study group and every time they went they said 'You should have been there, it was awesome. Come with us next time.' This pressured me to go with them and I did and I enjoyed the study group and got a lot out of it.
>
> Frances, 17

*I believe girls work best when they are with other girls
they feel comfortable with. It tends to make girls open and
imaginative.*

Haley, 15

*Girls learn best through discussion. If we aren't participating,
we aren't listening!*

Anon., 15

*Girls should discuss their ideas and topics for tests together,
but study and make notes on their own. I found if I studied
with my friends I got nothing done. I had to have peace
and quiet for a good two or three days to study at home
after school for a test on my own. Then I would share my
understanding by getting together with only one girl, usually
a study buddy, and we would go through the syllabus
comparing notes.*

Frances, 17

The interactive study sessions girls crave can be held at home or the local library – or they may well be virtual. Friends may get home from school, call each other and log on together. 'I keep telling Dad I need a bigger monitor, because I end up with so many windows open that I can't always follow what's going on in each one,' says one teenage girl. She and her best friend have about six different things going on at the same time, including multiple instant messaging screens for different friends, a virtual role-playing domain and 'The Palace', a site where users take on their own avatar – a character with its own unique identity – and communicate with other users' avatars. As well, 'we have our homework open (which, I'm pleased to report, we both get done at the end of the night, and it's soooo much more fun doing it this way!),' she says. Not to mention, of course, that they still have phone conversations going on at the same time.

It might seem alarming that girls are doing a lot of distracting things while they're meant to be doing their homework. Yet the scene this girl describes also sounds a lot like an average day at the office for most adults. We get our work done despite constant disruptions and the fact that we have to multi-task and keep our co-workers in the loop the whole time. To a certain extent, then, it's okay for girls to grow up learning and working in this way – so long as they know when to shut off distractions and work alone. If you work in an office, the equivalent might be that you know when it's time to close your office door, let the phone go to voicemail and wait until later to answer emails. When it comes to your daughter, it means touching base with her to make sure that she's got her tasks under control and is striking the right balance between networking, and spending time studying alone and completing assignments. Think of it as 'managed risk': giving your daughter the chance to self-manage how she learns, but being ready to step in and give her some boundaries if that isn't working out.

Reducing anxiety

It is crucial for teens to develop independence and make their own choices but they still need us to be there for them.

Teen girls flourish when their education challenges them, they have freedom to choose the course of their life, *and* they know that they can always rely on their family's unconditional love. 'Girls learn best when they have a neat balance of freedom and support,' says Lisa Porter, of Fairfield High School. 'They like to be challenged and have choice in what they do and how they learn, but they also need to feel scaffolded and supported, both in the classroom and at home.' When we gradually allow our girls more independence, while reassuring them that through thick and thin we will be there for them, we 'give them the confidence to really excel and be the best they can be,' says Lisa.

Carolyn Ryan, Adult Learning Liaison Officer at Dorrigo High School, in northern New South Wales, tells me that compared to boys the same age, girls at her school generally show greater multi-tasking and organising abilities. They develop time-management skills, such as the ability to do part-time work and still keep up with their study, and have better people skills, particularly an awareness of other people's needs. There is a risk to being good at these things, though. Being seen as proficient at handling everything, the girls are often left to do it all – even though they may end up feeling anxious and overwhelmed. 'They need strong support in their school or community group to ensure they aren't left with all the jobs,' Carolyn says. Girls need reassurance that the whole burden isn't on their shoulders. They should be encouraged to be assertive, to delegate to others and to expect other people to do their bit.

When girls are comfortable with their appearance and have a strong sense of self, they are better learners. They are prepared to take more risks and are less concerned about what others in the class might think of their work.

Lynne, teacher and mother of two girls, aged 14 and 16

Girls can be distracted very easily by interpersonal issues. Whether it's boys, friends or family, girls dwell on these relationships and quite often this can interfere with their learning. It's an unavoidable part of life, because even as adults we find ourselves distracted by such things, but girls need to have support at home to help them through those times.

Lisa Porter, Acting Head of Student Welfare, Fairfield High School, NSW

Choosing the right school

Choosing a school for your daughter can be stressful. Even after she has started at a school, you may wonder whether it is the right one. If you are in the midst of deciding on a school for your daughter or are re-evaluating her school, here are some of the things I recommend you look for.

School criteria

- **A positive school ethos.** Does the school's overall attitude mesh with your own outlook and beliefs about how your daughter should learn? Child and adolescent psychiatry expert Dr Brent Waters says, 'I am surprised that parents often look very closely at a school's reputation within the community and final Year 12 exam results, but don't always bother to have a closer look at the overall school ethos and ask whether or not it will focus on the development of the whole girl.'

- **Good learning experiences of students.** Excellent Year 12 final exam results are only one part of the puzzle when choosing a high school. For instance, does the school select or attract students who are more likely to receive excellent final exam results anyway, because of their social, educational or economic background? The real test is how much of a difference the high school actually makes to the students. Does the school enhance the students' learning or is it simply that by selecting or attracting bright students they inevitably get higher than average exam results?

- **Broad curriculum.** Look for schools that not only offer a wide variety of subjects but also encourage girls to feel confident to pursue all subjects, including ones traditionally thought of as masculine.

- **Strong student welfare policy.** Ideally your daughter's school should have a proactive student welfare policy rather than the 'tissue box' approach (handing out tissues to mop up the tears once things have gone wrong). Look for schools with programs that develop emotional intelligence and resilience, that run bullying prevention programs such as peer mentoring and peer mediation, and that have access to professionals such as school counsellors and the Police Youth Liaison team.

Find out, too, whether the school is set up so there is one particular teacher in the school who can know and care about your daughter; this may be a homeroom teacher or tutor.

- **Sexual harassment and violence policies.** Sexual harassment can take the form of assault or the sending of offensive and suggestive text messages. Find out what the school's policy is for dealing with this. What are they doing to prevent it? Similarly, find out whether violent assaults are a problem at the school and what they are doing to keep everyone safe.

- **Opportunities for student leadership.** Girls should be given as many chances as possible to try their hand at leadership, so look for a school where opportunities arise throughout every year of high school, not only the senior year when school captains are picked. Other leadership opportunities can come through student councils, clubs, teams and the mentoring of younger students, for instance.

- **Opportunities for parent involvement.** Even if you don't have the time to be directly involved, if a school has a strong partnership between staff and parents it is a good sign that it has a culture of openness and inclusiveness.

- **Learning support.** If your daughter is struggling with any of her subjects, are there specialists to give her extra assistance?

- **Community service programs.** Taking part in community service programs is wonderful for girls. They get to broaden their networks by interacting with people outside their usual school, home and friendship groups.

It reinforces the value of giving, in a society where we are so often obsessed with taking; and the value of community, in a world where the individual is usually the number one priority. Community service can create an awareness of global issues, a sense of justice, and the ability to empathise and care for others. Fourteen-year-old Laura told me: 'At my school it is cool to care about the Earth and people in poverty. This can always benefit our world.'

- **Extracurricular activities.** Activities offered by the school out of school hours can help your daughter find like-minded friends, develop her identity and build her self-esteem through success outside the classroom, so see whether the school offers a broad range of activities that your daughter may be interested in.

- **Vocational learning.** For vocational learning to be truly valuable, it should go beyond the traditional, and often tokenistic, one week's work experience. An excellent school takes the opportunity to make real-world connections in every lesson.

- **Staff quality.** The quality of a school's teaching staff has perhaps the biggest impact on learning. When I ask girls what the greatest barriers are to their learning, heading the list is 'teachers who don't know much about the subject they are teaching' (Emma, 15), 'if the teacher isn't very good' (Anon., 15), 'the way the teacher teaches' (Anon., 15), 'personality clash with teachers' (Felicity, 16), 'not liking teachers' (Kelly, 15), 'arguments with teachers' (Taryn, 16), 'what the teacher has said or done, because I get stubborn and won't do stuff for annoying teachers' (Aimee, 15), and on it goes. It may be hard for you to judge the quality of a school's teaching staff, but ask other parents with children at the school and make the most of opportunities to meet a school's teachers, say at an open day.

- **Staff retention.** Investigate further if you find that the teaching faculty at a school has undergone a lot of change, especially over a continuous period. This may be a sign of internal problems.
- **Fees.** If sending your daughter to a private school, be sure to stay well within your budget from the very beginning. Fees are likely to only increase, particularly in the senior years, and you don't want them becoming a burden.

When school becomes a problem

There may come a time when a problem arises for your daughter at school and you feel that one of her teachers is not successfully dealing with it, or is in fact the person causing the problem. This can be a highly emotional time, not only for your daughter but for you as well. But storming into her school, all guns blazing, is not going to resolve the situation. This is the time to take a deep breath, keep a clear head . . . and learn from the insiders. I asked a number of high school staff members to give their tips on how best to handle a problem at high school; the following is our combined advice.

The number one thing you need to do is get a very clear story from your daughter first. Wait until the dust has settled and both of you are a little less anxious and emotional, then find out exactly how she perceives the situation and what her grievances are, if any. Write notes if you feel that it will help you keep things clear in your mind. If you feel that a school policy has been broken by a student or staff member, look up the school's website or diary so you are certain of the school's policies.

Then, if you feel that you need to speak to the school about your concerns, phone the front office and ask for an appointment to meet with the teacher in person or have a discussion on the phone. Schools are busy places and teachers cannot run to the phone to take your call right away or – even worse – deal with a surprise visitor at their classroom door. Rather than phone the front office, you may prefer to email the teacher directly in order to ask for an appointment and that's fine, too. Just allow the teacher enough time to prepare for your appointment. 'In most schools, the year adviser can collect information from teachers about your child's behaviour, progress and overall wellbeing,' says Lisa Porter, of Fairfield High. She advises that you allow at least a week for the school to collect this information (or other relevant facts, depending on the issue).

When you do have your discussion with the school, make your complaint or concern as clear as possible, as calmly as possible. Then be sure to hear the school's staff out. Let them have a chance to give their side of the story, too. 'Be open-minded yet protective of your daughter,' is the advice of Margaret Taborda, Pastoral Care Co-ordinator and Social Justice Co-ordinator at Loreto Normanhurst, in Sydney. 'Most importantly, even if your daughter has done something really wrong, a good school would work with the parents, not against them.'

If you feel that your concerns are not being dealt with seriously, you may need to take it further, with another staff member. 'Explain this to the first person you are dealing with,' says Margaret Taborda, 'as sometimes the first person you talk to may not have the time or power to do something.'

If you have exhausted the options for resolving a problem with your daughter's school and she is miserable or you are seriously concerned about her education, safety or wellbeing, don't be afraid to change schools. I know it may sound drastic, but a student who is spiralling downward at one school may blossom if they change schools. Through my work with students at risk, I got to know a teenage boy who was on the verge of being expelled. The student wised up and realised he wanted to make a proper go of his schooling – but his old school was like poisoned ground for him, with teachers expecting him to behave badly and his friends pulling him back into his bad old ways. So he left his family in Sydney and went to live with his grandmother on the New South Wales north coast. The break was just what he needed. His results improved and within a year he was made captain of his new school.

Action plan
Keep the lines of communication open.
Show interest in your daughter's day at school – but understand she may be tired, hungry or just plain over it and may

not be very chatty when she first walks in the door. Rose, who is 13 years old, loves her mum but ends up having fights with her because 'when I get home from school she wants to talk to me and asks me about my day, and I am just tired, plus I have already lived it once and I don't want to live through it again'.

Also keep in mind that there are some things your daughter may not feel comfortable talking to you about. She may need 'an aunt, a big sister, counsellor or mentor,' says Lisa Porter, of Fairfield High School. 'Please don't be hurt if it's not you she turns to every time. It doesn't mean she doesn't love you! She might not want to worry you.'

Help your daughter learn to manage her own workload.
If your daughter has trouble getting assignments finished on time, completing her homework or revising for exams, sit down with her and help her to work out ways to get on top of her studies. As adults, we know how to keep track of everything – well, most of the time – but girls sometimes need a helping hand at mastering this skill. It can be as simple as showing your daughter how to make effective use of diaries and calendars, or how to make lists of her tasks then tick them off one by one.

Help her develop good study techniques.
Most schools provide lessons in study techniques but if your daughter is struggling with how best to do assignments, make summaries or revise for exams, talk to her school to see if they have any extra resources. You may want to consider using a study skills program outside of the school. If

your daughter develops the fundamental skills for studying, it will be worth the investment. Resist the temptation to do your daughter's assignments. You may feel that you are helping her but the benefit will be short term; and if she doesn't develop good study skills herself, she will have more problems in the long term.

Encourage informed risk-taking.
When your daughter wants to try something new at school – a different subject, joining the debating team, trying out for the school musical – give her positive feedback for taking a chance, even if the outcome isn't a success. This is a time when your daughter can explore new fields and see what she really is interested in and good at. She may make a few mistakes along the way or suffer some setbacks, but learning to deal with disappointment is part of growing up.

Highlight the achievements of learned women.
I confess that I once said to my daughter when she was struggling with maths, 'You're just like your mummy. We both love reading and writing but find maths and science tough.' Way to go, Danni. What kind of message was I sending Teyah? The same message Mattel's Barbie gave girls when she spoke her first words in 1992: 'Math class is tough!' How limiting. Throughout history there have been accomplished women across all fields of learning. Take every opportunity to remind your daughter of the many women who have achieved academically. Help her seek out textbooks that depict women participating in scientific

discoveries, the literary world and political events. What were all those women doing while the men were off exploring, anyway? When your daughter has a choice, encourage her to choose women authors or heroines for her assignments and book projects.

Even the most-simple empowering message you give your teen daughter can have a lasting effect on her. Fifteen years ago, Rachel, who is now a grown woman, was in a class I taught at high school. She says, 'I still remember the first thing I noticed when I walked into your classroom in Year 10: a sticker on the top of the board that said "Girls can be engineers too." Yours was one of the few classrooms where I believed that I could achieve something.'

Get tech savvy.
It is essential that all young people start secondary school with at least basic computing skills. If your daughter is struggling, enrol her in a short course privately. You may even want to enrol with her.

Bring back balance.
Some of the learning obstacles girls frequently mention are lack of sleep, hunger and stress. I am sure everyone would agree it's lamentable that teenagers are already suffering from these pressures. But many working women would probably nominate similar problems as our greatest barriers to a good day's work. Rather than lamenting this, though, we tend to shrug it off as just something we have to put up with. To be at your best, both you and your daughter need a good night's sleep, a balanced diet and stress management

(for more on that, see Appendix 2). The most effective way to encourage your daughter to lead a more balanced and sustaining lifestyle is to try to live that way *with* her.

Affirmations

I enjoy learning new things.

I have the potential to achieve and I have

faith in my abilities.

9

Career Girl

⸙

After appearing on *60 Minutes* one night to talk about the work I do empowering teen girls, I took part in an online chat session with viewers. One concerned person asked me: 'Are you breeding little feminists, though?'

I responded then as I would now: 'I hope so!'

'Feminism' has become the new f-word – an insult, a word not to be spoken in polite company. All the time, I hear young women say things like 'I'm not a feminist, but . . .'

Feminism is the belief that women deserve equality. Is that really *so* radical a concept that we feel the need to disavow it?

Perhaps it is because women have made such enormous progress towards gaining equality and respect in society. When our teenage daughters enter the workforce, they won't come up against the rigid barriers that existed mere decades ago, when a woman's future was all mapped out for her. School, work for a few years, marriage, babies and house-work – for generations of girls that was the plan, whether it was the life they dreamed of or not. Our girls have choices. They will inherit laws against gender discrimination and sexual harassment, and laws protecting a woman's right to keep her job after having a baby. Believing that the work of feminism is complete in this country, perhaps women feel that the f-word is an embarrassing throwback to a bygone era and should be allowed to slip out of our vocabulary.

Not so fast!

Our daughters *will* still face barriers when they enter the workplace. The same barriers that we have been trying to chip away at, bit by bit, all our adult lives. These are barriers that no government can smash down, no court of law can rule out of existence. They're more shadowy and hard to pin down than that. The obstacles that our teenage daughters will face exist largely in people's minds. They're the mis-conceptions that employers have about women and about men; stereotyped ideas of what is women's work and what is men's; inflexible attitudes towards childcare; a workplace culture that doesn't offer a home/work balance; an ingrained lack of confidence that holds too many girls and women back from showing their true talents or from negotiating in the workplace as successfully as they could.

These misconceptions and stereotypes are why women's

pay still lags behind men's. On average, the weekly pay a woman takes home is 84 per cent of a man's. The imbalance is right there from the beginning: when a young man graduates from a tertiary degree he can expect a median salary of $45,000 while a young woman graduate can expect to start out on $42,000. That pattern is carried through right up to senior levels of business, with the median wage of a woman chief financial officer being 51 percent less than her male counterparts'. (I had to run my eye back over that figure again, too, certain I'd misread it the first time.) A clue that may help explain the chasm between men's and women's pay is the fact that women remain massively under-represented at the upper levels of the business world. Out of all 200 companies that make up the Australian stock market index known as the ASX 200, there were only six women CEOs in 2006. Finally, and unsurprisingly, women are far more likely than men to be sexually harassed or discriminated against in the workplace.

If wanting to redress these imbalances makes me a feminist, then I am delighted to be called one. My idea of feminism welcomes anyone who supports the notion that women are people with rights, and that all people deserve an equal opportunity in life. Guys are definitely invited to join, too.

Even if you don't fancy ever using the f-word yourself, I know you want the best for your daughter's future. Young people are given a lot of information when considering their options, along with a whole lot of pressure to choose the right subjects at school, the right tertiary course or the right career path. Many teenage girls I speak with are overwhelmed about sifting through work and study possibilities, meanwhile weighing up the benefits and pitfalls of taking a part-time job while they are still at school. This chapter is devoted to what you can do to help your daughter find her own way through the maze. It looks at what holds some young women back from the career success they deserve and what we can do to help our girls (and ourselves) find fulfilment in our working lives. It celebrates all the amazing talents and qualities this generation of teen girls and women have to offer, and suggests how we can enhance them and share them with the world.

The best part of being a teenage girl is having more responsibilities and finding out about the real outside world.

Jessica, 15

Being a teenage girl gives me the opportunity to begin discovering who I am before I enter the scary, yet hopefully exciting, world of adulthood.

Kirsten, 17

The best part of being a teenage girl is having a whole future and the best part of your life ahead of you.

Amy, 16

Welcome to the boys' club

A high-powered job isn't everyone's cup of tea. Some women choose to devote themselves to parenting full-time, which is surely the hardest job on Earth; others are in the workforce but have no interest in pursuing a senior role. But there are also women who would like to be in the country's board-rooms and in managerial positions but find their careers stalling. The fact that women are grossly under-represented in the upper levels of our workplaces is not simply due to women choosing other roles. In fact, the federal govern-ment's Equal Opportunity for Women in the Workplace Agency (EOWA) conducted research among both sexes in the workforce and found that men and women are equally ambitious. In significant numbers, both sexes believe that in their workplace men progress more quickly than women, that promotions are not always awarded on merit, and that women and men are not treated equally. In many cases, the Australian workplace is a boys' club. Almost half of all working women think so: 43 per cent. What might surprise you is that the number of men who perceive their workplace as a boy's club is even greater: 46 per cent.

Women often feel that in order to get recognition they need to work harder than men doing the same job. Excluded from the boys' club, it can be harder for them to progress. One woman surveyed summed up the experience of many women when she said that the men at her work 'stick together to promote each other' while the women were left to 'fight battles on their own'.

The boys' club workplace culture makes it easier for men to get away with discriminating against or sexually harass-ing their female co-workers. We have all heard outrageous stories of harassment or have lived through it ourselves: a woman who fails to get a job after an interview and instead scores a proposition from her male interviewer; a woman who is offered a promotion only to find the offer withdrawn when she announces she's pregnant; a woman who is subjected to ridicule when she asks that men take down the porno magazine pictures plastered all over their workspaces. Bullying and harassment can come at the hands of women, too. Women's snide comments to other women in the workplace are destructive: 'You must be sleeping with him' or 'It helps that you have great legs,' a woman may say to a female colleague on her promotion. The EOWA survey found that a staggering one in ten women left their last job because they suffered bullying or harassment. Teen girls, with their relative inexperience and lack of power in the workplace, are especially vulnerable.

The need is as great now as it ever was for girls and women to support and stand up for one another in the workplace.

Working mum: money-maker, chief cook and bottle-washer

Almost every adult in the workforce feels they need to spend more time at home with their family than they currently do. They feel burdened by financial responsibilities and demanding workloads that keep them away from the people they love and the non-work activities that keep them sane. We know this not only from our own conversations with other busy working adults, but from research as well. Women are not alone in feeling the ache of wanting to spend more time at home. One survey showed that almost 70 per cent of men feel they don't spend enough time with their children. Another found that 60 per cent feel that they miss out on some of the rewards of being a father because of their jobs.

Despite the fact that both men and women yearn to spend more time at home with their family, when they are at home, women and men are doing very different things with their time. Working women are working not only at their jobs but at home as well. Women continue to do most of the cooking, laundering, nappy-changing, bathing, dressing, grooming, grocery shopping, and the organising of a million and one soccer or netball games, music lessons, birthday parties, school recitals, doctor's appointments and so on in the family. Women with partners spend almost 30 hours each week on household duties. Their men? They spend around half as much time on housework. Even in couples where both partners work full-time, women spend around seven hours more each week on household activities. Emily Maguire writes, in her book *Princesses and Pornstars*:

> While the professional and legal positions of women have improved enormously in the last half-century, socially and domestically, we've barely progressed at all. We are still judged first on how well we conform to gendered norms that were already looking tattered in 1955. In spite of a need for it, we continually hear that feminism is a thing of the past.

In the norms she is referring to, women are the homemakers and men are the breadwinners. We can get stuck in a self-perpetuating cycle. Carrying a greater burden of caring and housework at home, we may have less energy to focus on the direction of our careers. Men, expected to take on fewer burdens at home, may be better placed to take advantage of promotions and new opportunities, possibly leaving their women with even more to do at home.

This has to stop, not only for our own careers but for our daughters' futures. Our children learn by watching what we do, which means that for change to come about we need to set the right example at home, for our daughters *and our sons*. If you have a partner who doesn't do his fair share, change the conversation: make it about the future of your kids. Get your children involved in doing their bit, with chores equally spread between boys and girls. If you are parenting on your own, take whatever help that is available. Too long we have been focused on being superwomen who can do it all, the subtext being that we *should* do it all.

> There are pressures on me to balance my very demanding role with parenting. Human rights start at home! I believe doing work I value makes me a better mother and a strong role model for Lucy. I try to make home a guilt-free zone.
>
> Elizabeth Broderick, Sex Discrimination Commissioner and Commissioner responsible for Age Discrimination

> Employers that mistakenly avoid recruiting women based on the inaccurate stereotypes about [women] and the impact that caring responsibilities can have on their careers risk overlooking some of the best talent in the Australian workforce.
>
> Equal Opportunity for Women in the Workplace Agency

Career girl: playground bully, saint or style icon?

I do not buy women's magazines. I gave up that self-destructive little habit some time ago because I got sick of the nasty aftertaste: I really am not coping as well as *[insert celebrity mum]*, am I? Wow, I had no idea I could/should lose three kilos by next week! Maybe I do need to update my wardrobe . . .

However, on a business trip I decided to dive back into that world and before my flight picked up a copy of *Vive*, a magazine 'for women who mean business'. What sage advice for businesswomen did I find in those 128 pages?

– Fifteen different types of wrinkle cream were advertised or discussed (yes, I counted) including the $930 La Prairie Pure Gold product featuring 'finely ground 24-carat gold'. (Why use gold? Because we can?)

– There was a four-page feature story on Kelly Smythe, a stylist at Channel 7. She sounds like a talented, hard-working woman. My problem with the story was its implication that the main reason Channel 7 was rating well was that the stars now all 'dressed for success' and that Kelly was there to 'keep a check' on how they all looked. Surely there is more to success than just the right pantsuit?

– There was a profile of ex-supermodel and now France's first lady, Carla Bruni, whose main claim to fame, according to the magazine, seemed to be that she 'once dated Mick Jagger and Eric Clapton'. *Vive* claimed there was more to Bruni than just her love life – but if so, why did they mention it? Repeatedly.

– The model in the magazine's fashion spread looked

no older than 15. Physically, she appeared prepubescent: flat-chested, all long, gangling limbs, and wearing a seventies-inspired playsuit and enormous retro wedges in one shot. Oh, how 'career girl'! If the editor knew her demographic – and by the looks of all that anti-wrinkle-cream advertising, the mag is targeting over-35s – what was she hoping to achieve with this spread, other than a feeling of crippling inadequacy in her readers?

– The recipe section (you know this must be a magazine for *women* who mean business because you won't see a recipe section in the boy's own *Business Review Weekly*) featured silly, fiddly hors d'oeuvres. What working woman has time to whip up 'mulloway and caviar tartare'? 'Iberico ham and quail-egg tarts'? I particularly resented the magazine's guilt-loaded message that crackers and cheese were now a definite no-no and that even 'risotto balls are considered passé.' Blimey, don't come here for nibbles, then.

I could go on and on. Don't even get me started on the tokenistic story on what feminism means today, buried up on page 114 and entitled 'The F-word'.

The f-word that came to mind for me when reading this magazine was . . . frivolous.

Success in the business world is not about having youthful skin, a stick-thin figure, name-droppable boyfriends, stylish clothes and the ability to whip up a marvellous quail-egg tart. So where are the images in popular culture of *real* successful business and career women? Boys are saturated with images of working men to model themselves on, in movies, children's stories, novels, TV shows, news coverage, ads. They have had fathers from generation to generation passing down their expectations of the kind of working man they are to be. But women and girls are, to a large extent, still making up the working-woman identity as we go along. This can lead us to inadvertently set up our own traps to be snared in at work. With few role models and scant advice, women may one minute try to live up to their imaginary idea of a hard-nosed businesswoman, then revert to playground cattiness or fall back on the old lessons of our girlhood, when we got rewarded for being sugar and spice and all things nice.

Saintly traits that tend to be expected of women – such as being humble, selfless and passive – can also put us at a disadvantage in the workplace. Deborah Rhode, an expert on gender equality at Stanford University, in the United States, writes: 'Many traits traditionally valued of women also perpetuate women's inequality.' As an antidote, above my desk I display a quote from Marianne Williamson's classic book *A Return to Love*:

> There is nothing enlightening about shrinking so that
> other people will not feel insecure around you . . . and as
> we let our light shine, we unconsciously give other people
> permission to do the same. As we are liberated from our
> own fear, our presence liberates others.

It is important for all us women to be proud of our talents and abilities, and become more comfortable discussing our achievements. This will not only help us in our career and life, it will also encourage our girls to be upfront about their skills, which will assist them in being more assertive. We need to show girls that it is okay to actively promote themselves and that, in fact, it is essential if they are to reach their full potential.

Women in the workplace tend to find it difficult to assert their worth to others. We find it tough to tell our employers and other workplace power players that we deserve recognition, respect, a raise or a promotion. We fear looking vain or like a diva, and worry that we'll be perceived as a bitch or full of ourselves. We hate to risk being disliked. Advertisers know women tend to like wearing good clothes and bling because they signal to the world 'Hey, I'm worth it!' Yet at work, we have trouble telling employers and colleagues exactly that: I am skilled and experienced and deserve your respect.

We are living in a highly competitive business era in which the employment market has been transformed by intense competition for jobs as well as the introduction of individual workplace agreements. It will only become more important that you and your daughter feel comfortable about promoting your skills and negotiating with others. You don't know your market value until you ask, and expect, to be paid well for good work.

The entitled generation

If only finding the right career was a matter of deciding what we want to be then clicking our ruby-red heels together. Finding a job that suits us and gives us a sense of fulfilment and satisfaction can be a long journey. There may be twists and turns, long, flat boring plains, splendid, scenic peaks and dismal chasms. Along the way we inevitably have to do our share of dull tasks and learn many lessons. Then maybe forget them and learn them all over again. Even if we get our dream job, we may find that it wasn't really our destination at all but only a detour, and that now we have a different goal and completely different things to learn.

Most of us learnt these truths early on, way back when we got a part-time job during high school. The expectations of this generation are quite different, though. Some girls I meet now have a sense of entitlement more suited to a 30-something executive. I meet girls who can't see why they should have to start out at the bottom and work their way up. Not all girls – but enough to get my antennae twitching.

I can honestly say that I have loved every job I ever had, including working as a babysitter, restaurant waitress and at McDonald's. Each job has taught me something valuable. At McDonald's, for instance, I learnt how to work in a team, motivate and train colleagues, and look after customers. I also developed a strong work ethic there, because the job demanded that I work hard. Girls with a feeling of entitlement believe they shouldn't need to do such gritty starter jobs because it's beneath them. What they don't realise is how much they are missing out on. They will lag behind other girls in learning fundamental skills crucial to success in the workplace later on. And their attitude may be a big turn-off to potential employers.

Mia Freedman, who became editor of *Cosmopolitan* at the tender age of 24, didn't just roll out of bed into a great outfit and killer heels then step into that position, as too many girls of the entitled generation feel they should be able to. She started her career doing work experience as an ambitious 19-year-old, and was happy to fetch the mail and get coffee at first. If she had the chance to fill in for the receptionist at lunch, she was rapt, happy simply to be there 'breathing the air'. When she did become an editor, she made a special effort with other young people who came in for work experience looking for a way into the competitive world of magazine publishing. 'I insisted we have a structured program to give them a well-rounded understanding of how a magazine worked,' she writes.

> Inevitably, this included some boring tasks because – *guess what kids* – there are many, many boring tasks to be done in every workplace. At every level.
>
> Over the years, I began to notice a change in attitude from some (not all) of the work experience students. Gratitude was being replaced with a sense of entitlement and absurd expectations.

Years later, after leaving the magazine game, she was flicking through the newspaper one morning and was shocked to see she'd been mentioned in an article featuring other magazine editors:

> The gist of the story was that the magazine industry was apparently in a 'tizz' about some anonymous rumours on a website.
>
> One of these rumours – are you sitting down? – was that '*Mia Freedman once sent a work experience person out to buy her son a banana.*'

This is but one of many examples of work experience students and junior staff members chafing at being asked to do tasks that they feel are beneath them. One of Mia's friends asked a young person to help a fashion assistant carry some clothes. They refused, delivering the immortal line 'I have a degree, I'm not a Sherpa.'

There is good self-esteem – and then there is this unfounded preciousness that seems more like narcissism. We need to support our girls' sense of self-worth, but not at the expense of giving them a true grounding in reality. Most career women at the top of their game have years of hard slogging, networking and persistence behind them.

Even women who choose to work in some of the industries widely considered to be glamorous have had to put in their time doing work that is anything but glamorous. Melinda Nielsen is one of Australia's premier make-up artists and styles major celebrities. 'Long before I even studied makeup you could find me working on the makeup counters,' she says. 'Those years were truly my foundation for what I am doing now. It's where I really learnt my craft because . . . it gave me a vast array of experience not only with applying make-up but also in building relationships with people.' After gaining qualifications, many of her fellow students didn't know where to go from there and floundered, struggling to find a foothold in the highly competitive industry.

'I hold a personal belief that you become like the people you hang around,' says Melinda, 'so I found people who were successful . . . I began to assist with some of the top make-up artists in Australia. I did whatever it took to be in their world – I cleaned brushes, carried bags and got some fantastic opportunities. I started making my own contacts and building relationships, and that launched me into my career.'

Sophie York, barrister, lecturer, author and mother of four concurs: 'One of my first jobs was as a shopkeeper . . . I was pressured initially to do work as a paralegal yet I have no regrets over my choice as through this starter role I learnt so much about human nature and people. Working where I did I was exposed to a side of life I had had limited contact with previously – homeless people, drug addicts – and it helped me develop a stronger sense of compassion and empathy which I brought to my later work in the legal profession.'

Hard junior-level work is not necessarily a bad thing. Even tasks that seem 'beneath' your daughter can teach her valuable skills, not to mention impress employers who are looking for staff with a good attitude. However, your daughter should not allow herself to be exploited. If she is asked to do things that make her feel uncomfortable or that are dangerous or wildly inappropriate, she should be encouraged to question such requests and to set boundaries.

Which career?

Only your daughter herself can make the tough decisions about what she wants to do when she leaves school, but there are ways that you can help her. You are your daughter's greatest role model so don't be surprised to find that she may turn to you to find out how you made study and career decisions. Offering up your experiences – good and bad – may help her make her own choices. A natural, ongoing two-way dialogue is important here, rather than a lecture. Your role is to help her find the right path *for her*, so keep an open mind.

Get to know what jobs your daughter is interested in and then think about ways you can help her find out more about them. If you know someone who has a job your daughter is interested in, see if you can set up a time for them to meet so she can ask how they got into the field and what the pros and cons are. Hands-on experience is the best way to learn about a job – and it looks good on a CV – so if there is a chance for your daughter to do some work at your friend's workplace, whether paid or unpaid, encourage her to try it. The activities your teenager is involved in outside of school, such as sports and hobbies, can also be a useful clue for the kind of work they will be suited to. Maybe your daughter even has a special skill or talent that could be nurtured and lead to a career.

Getting to know what your daughter *isn't* interested in is just as valuable. One of the key lessons I have learnt is that just because you *can* do something, it doesn't mean you *should*. This is a trap that young women fresh out of school can be easily led into: excited and flattered to be offered a great job, they do it even though their heart and soul are somewhere else. Other girls take a highly sought-after place at university such as medicine simply because they got the marks and are excited that they won that race. Melinda Nielsen notes that 'it is very important to be talented at what you do, but it will never be enough to succeed in a competitive field. Firstly, I think you need to have a passion for what you are doing, otherwise you will lose hope when the setbacks start to come. If you are passionate about something you will want to persevere with it and won't give up when it gets tough.'

So don't neglect the signs of what jobs are uninspiring for your daughter, too. If she tries her hand at a part-time job or a work-experience placement and really doesn't like or do well at it, try discussing what it was about the work that was a turn-off for her, as this can help her pinpoint the right career.

Don't overlook the resources available at school and in the community, too. Making a time for you and your daughter to speak to her school career adviser can be a great place to start, as can career expos.

What if my daughter wants to leave school early?

When I was in high school, about a third of the students left at the end of Year 10 to work full time. The majority of my friends left at this point and went on to have fabulous careers. However, the world has definitely changed since then and satisfying full-time job opportunities for early school leavers just don't exist any more. Most teenagers can find only part-time work and people aged 15 to 24 have almost three times the level of unemployment of those aged 24 to 54. Today, young people should aim to complete their first year of senior schooling or an equivalent vocational qualification, as an absolute minimum.

Your daughter may complain that the learning she does at school is not relevant and say that she will be happier in the 'real world'. There *are* many 'unreal' elements to schooling – but it is those very elements that can be of enormous benefit for teens. School is a generally nurturing environment that allows young people to make mistakes; the real world is not always so kind. Students desperate to leave school often come back to visit a few months later and say they are filled with regret about their decision as they feel lost and lonely in their new workplace. They miss their friends and being able to interact with other young people all day.

'I think for girls who leave school early it is challenging, as they don't really fit in anywhere,' says Leigh, whose daughter left early to go to business college. 'Her school friends all bonded over exams and playground gossip, which of course she was no longer a part of, whilst the other girls she worked with in the office [were] much older . . . For a while there, she didn't seem to fit socially anywhere.'

In the end, the choice is in your daughter's hands. If she is adamant about leaving school early, encourage her to consider combining school studies with some practical, paid training. There are a number of Vocational Education and Training (VET) programs that can be studied at school or by correspondence.

What skills are important in today's workplace?

There is no such thing as a job for life any more and our daughters are likely to move through several different careers in their working lives, just like many of us. This means that to succeed in the modern workplace, we need to make sure we develop the basic skills and qualities that employers across a broad spectrum of jobs will always look for. This list of employability skills is based on one compiled by the Department of Education, Science and Training, the Australian Chamber of Commerce and Industry, and the Business Council of Australia.

The 8 employability skills

- **Communication** – listening and understanding other staff and customers; speaking and writing clearly; being assertive
- **Learning** – applying learning to practical situations; being willing to learn in any setting; managing your own learning
- **Technology** – having basic technology skills; being willing to learn about new technology
- **Teamwork** – working well with people of different ages, gender, race and religion; working well as an individual and as a team member
- **Planning and organising** – managing time and priorities; coordinating with others; planning; collecting and organising information
- **Problem solving** – developing creative, innovative solutions to problems; using mathematics to solve problems
- **Self-management** – managing your own time and priorities; taking initiative; making decisions
- **Enterprise** – adapting to new situations; being resourceful and creative; identifying new opportunities

The personal qualities employers prize the most are loyalty, reliability, commitment, honesty, integrity, enthusiasm, a sense of justice and care for others, the ability to deal with pressure, motivation, adaptability, good personal presentation, common sense, positive self-esteem and a sense of humour.

Young people wanting to start their own businesses need to understand more than just the mechanics of the corporate world; they need confidence to use their whole, creative selves in their working lives, to employ their hopes and aspirations, to pursue their passions. Creativity is the central, challenging part of business . . .

I'd also like to see entrepreneurial – as distinct from managerial – skills taught to young people. But above all we have a responsibility to teach children to think critically, to distinguish information from entertainment, advertisement and political propaganda, and to trust and develop their intuitive selves.

Leanne Preston, founder of the company Wild Child, and 2007
Telstra Australian Business Woman of the Year

It is because of the relationships that I've built that I've had most of the opportunities and open doors throughout my career. Be genuine in your dealings with people. Most people have a pretty good radar for detecting a fake. So be real. Treat people the way you would like to be treated, even if it's difficult to do so. This will build in you resilience and strength of character, which are always great qualities to have.

Melinda Nielsen, make-up artist

Action plan

The ideas in this action plan are targeted towards helping your daughter choose her career path, but you may find them equally helpful if you are re-entering the workforce or reassessing the direction of your career.

Start an Employability Skills Portfolio.
This is a record of the ways in which your daughter has demonstrated the eight employability skills at school, at home or in part-time work, both paid and unpaid. I suggest you introduce this idea to your daughter as early as possible and set it up for her as a document that she can update regularly. For example, under 'Planning and organising' your daughter could note a school group assignment in which she had to allocate tasks to the other group members; forming a band outside of school, for which she recruited new members; and organising a children's birthday party at her part-time job at a fast-food chain.

Regularly updating a skills portfolio will increase your daughter's confidence; and when the time comes for her to apply for work, she will have a wealth of evidence of her achievements and skills at her fingertips. Reinforce the importance of the employability skills at home from an early age. Explain that doing her share of family chores is not only a decent thing to do but also a great way to develop her teamwork, and planning and organising skills.

Mothers who start their own skills portfolio feel empowered by it. When looking for employment or seeking a promotion, having a skills portfolio can be very helpful. Knowing the skills employers are looking for, and having evidence that we have developed those skills, allows us to speak the same language when we go to a job interview or salary review.

When I look at the skills portfolios of the girls and women I work with, I feel optimistic about their opportunities. Many of the skills and personal attributes employers look for relate to emotional intelligence and research has shown this is an area women tend to be strong in: we are naturally inclined to have strong relationship skills and to be good at managing our emotions and those of others. Developing better self-esteem and assertiveness not only helps us feel better about ourselves, it helps make us more employable!

Nurture your daughter's growing independence.
An alarming number of parents look for jobs for their teenage children, scouring job boards and making calls on their children's behalf. Please don't be tempted to do this. Your daughter needs to learn to become independent and manage her career herself. If she is going to fumble or stumble, it is better that she does so now, not in her twenties, when the stakes are higher. And imagine if you were an employer and received a call from a candidate's mum; it's unlikely you would think of that teen as mature or high in initiative.

Put together a great CV.
Employers may get hundreds of applications every time they advertise a position. They do not want to wade through too much information; nor do they want a CV that's difficult to read. A CV should be no longer than two pages and typed in a simple 12-point font, in black and white. Your daughter

should include the following on her CV.

Key CV points

- **Contact details** – If your daughter has a frivolous-sounding email address such as partyprincess@hotmail.com, encourage her to set up a second, more professional one she can use for job applications
- **Career Objective** – A few simple words such as 'To be employed in a stimulating environment where I can make a positive contribution and share my enthusiasm for learning and working with others'
- **Education** – First should come her current year of schooling and the subjects she is studying. Then she should list any training courses, e.g. first aid, word processing
- **Awards** – These should include not only academic achievements but any significant awards for extracurricular activities such as sport or dance
- **Employment** – All paid and unpaid jobs or work experience
- **Interests** – Your daughter should think carefully about how she describes her interests, e.g. 'live music and dancing' sounds much better than 'going to raves'
- **Key skills** – The key skills mentioned in the job advertisement should be addressed here. This is where the Employability Skills Portfolio proves invaluable, as your daughter can refer back to it. For example, if the ad mentions that applicants need strong communication skills, one of the points in the 'Key skills' section of the CV might read:

Communication

At school I have participated in a wide variety of activities that have helped me develop both my written and my verbal communication skills, including debating, public speaking, letter writing and producing essays. While working as a volunteer for the RSPCA, I assisted in handing out pamphlets to members of the public and advised them on how to best care for their pets. The staff at the RSPCA always enjoyed talking to me and I liked explaining information to pet owners of various ages and backgrounds.

- **Referees** – Written references are becoming rare, so contact details should be supplied of two or three responsible adults who can vouch for your daughter in a workplace (in a paid or unpaid position), at school or in a group she belongs to such as a sporting or debating team.

Don't neglect the cover letter.

The cover letter is the first impression an employer has of your daughter. Like her CV, it needs to be clear and simple, not busy or decorated. It should be concise and to the point – definitely no longer than a page – and should briefly illustrate how she fulfils the requirements listed in the job ad. Increasingly, jobs are advertised online without the name of a contact person. In such a case, encourage your daughter to call the organisation and find the name of the person who will be making the hiring decision, and address the cover letter to that person. When that is not possible, she should avoid the informal Internet-age greeting 'Hi' and use instead 'Dear Human Resources' or 'Dear Hiring Manager'.

Prepare for the job interview.
The key is preparation. Your daughter needs to learn how to get ready for a job interview independently, so this is another one of those times when as mothers we need to be there to offer guidance and support, not do it all for her. A checklist may help your daughter feel more organised and on top of everything when she goes to the interview.

Pre-interview checklist

- **Learn about the company** – What does the organisation make or sell, or what service does it provide?
- **Learn about the job** – What will you be required to do in the job and where does the role fit into the organisation?
- **Get your employment file ready** – Make sure you have a presentation folder to take with you to the interview, containing:
  - CV
  - Cover letter you sent to apply for this job
  - Qualifications and school records
  - Certificates or special awards relevant to the job
  - Written references, if you have them
  - Samples of your work or hobbies that may be related to the job
- **Know how to get there**
  - Double-check the address of the organisation

- Look up how to get there
- Check public transport timetables or parking options, aiming to arrive at least 10 minutes early
- If in doubt, do a trial run and time how long it takes
- **Plan how you'll present yourself**
  - Decide what you are going to wear and have it ready the night before. Dress to suit the occasion. Avoid wearing 'way out' clothes, scruffy jeans or thongs
  - Be clean, neat and tidy. Brush your hair, have clean fingernails (no chipped nail polish) and clean shoes
- **Practise your answers** – Be prepared to give brief, clear answers to questions that employers commonly ask in interviews:
  - What aspects of the job interest you most?
  - What do you consider your special skills and abilities are?
  - Have you had any work experience in this type of work?
  - What do you know about our company?
  - Are you active in any clubs or community organisations?
  - What are your leisure activities, hobbies or interests?
  - Which of your school subjects interested you the most?
  - What are your long-term career plans?
  - Would you undertake further training if it was required for this position?
  - How do you cope with new situations and procedures?
  - How do you feel about working as part of a team?
  - Would you be prepared to work overtime or on weekends if required?
  - When could you start?

- **Practise your questions** – If invited by the employer to ask questions, ask job-related questions rather than, say, questions about holidays or pay. This creates a good impression and lets the employer know you are eager to work for the company. Examples include:
  - What would my career prospects be?
  - What further study could I do?
  - Where and whom would I be working with?
  - Is any training given with the position?

Ace the job interview.

Unless your daughter has nerves of steel, there is a good chance she will feel nervous and a little uncertain. These tips may help.

Job interview tips

- Arrive 10 minutes early, to give yourself time to gather your thoughts and check your appearance
- Switch off your mobile phone
- Introduce yourself to the receptionist. Give your name, time of the appointment and the name of the person who is interviewing you. Speak clearly and politely. When the receptionist tells you where to wait, thank them and wait quietly.
- Greet the interviewer(s) and introduce yourself.
- Smile and be ready to shake hands
- Enter the interviewer's office and wait to take the seat that is offered to you
- Maintain eye contact, as this shows you are listening

and that you are confident and trustworthy
- Though you may be nervous, make sure you keep your hands and legs still. Don't fidget or fiddle. Don't even think about smoking or chewing gum!
- Answer questions honestly, politely and clearly, and in sufficient detail
- Always try to turn the question to your advantage. This is your opportunity to show you have the skills, interests and experience to do the job
- Don't be shy about your achievements. No achievement is too small to mention, if it is relevant to a question that the interviewer has asked
- If you don't understand a question, ask for clarification. That is better than risking an irrelevant answer
- Try not to punctuate your sentences with 'umm' or 'err' or 'like'. Taking a short pause to think about the question is perfectly acceptable and makes a much better impression
- At the end of the interview, politely thank the interviewer(s).

Review progress after every interview.
It may seem that a job interview is a win–lose proposition. Get the job = win. Get knocked back = lose. A more helpful way to look at an unsuccessful job interview is as a learning opportunity. After each interview, encourage your daughter to evaluate her performance. What does she think she did well? What does she feel she could improve on next time? An unsuccessful interview is not a waste of time but an experience she can reflect on to help in future interviews.

Make the most of work experience.

It is important that your daughter knows she won't be given the most challenging or glamorous tasks during work experience. She won't be standing up in court saying 'I object!' during her week at a law firm; she may well be fetching the mail or tidying up the boardroom. Nevertheless, by being proactive your daughter can get the maximum value out of her work experience. If she finds herself shunted to the Siberian outer reaches of the office, given nothing constructive to do, she can approach the person who is supervising her work experience and politely say something such as 'I would really like to build on my employment skills this week. Is there anything you would like me to do that could help me develop them?' Having a copy of the eight employability skills in hand will give the work experience supervisor something concrete to go on.

Don't reject volunteer work as a valuable means of gaining both experience and making connections. Sophie York firmly believes it was some of the unpaid opportunities she embraced early on that allowed her not only to network with mentors who had time to share their wisdom, but also eventually led her to interesting, well-paid positions:

'One of the things I think is really invaluable in the early days is to seek out other people who have gone before you. In the workplace it can be hard to find people who have the time to be nurturing, so I sought mentors through volunteer positions that connected young people with retired professionals who had been there, done that. The key, too, is to think: What can I offer? What can I contribute? Don't make money the priority – make learning and service the priority.

If you do this, the money will come. For example, early on in my career I volunteered as a magistrate at a university for their students' mock trial exercises. This later led to the offer of paid lecturing work at that university which in turn led to other wonderful things too.'

Be proud of yourself and your achievements.
As always, one of the best things you can do to help your daughter is to be a good role model. Take pride in whatever work it is that you do. Check yourself when one of the many phrases that women use in conversation to downplay their achievements pops out, such as 'I'm just a stay-at-home mum . . .' or 'It was nothing, anyone could have done it . . .' When you value your own achievements, you give your daughter permission to value her own.

Affirmations
I have a bounty of skills and talents
to offer the world.
Whatever work I choose to do,
I do it well and learn from it.

Conclusion

Don't Hold Back

❦

So often when I ask for girls' feedback after an Enlighten Education workshop they begin by saying they thought it would be 'just another self-esteem talk' or 'boring lecture'. Invariably they go on to say how much more it was. They say they loved the way we made them feel; they loved us; they were inspired by the power of the love we showed them.

I am still, and will always be, changed by it. It was the only real thing I have ever done in my life. Danni, your honesty and integrity and the rawness of your love for us made it large.

Toni, 16

At first I was surprised by the prevalence of the word 'love' in the girls' feedback. Such a bold world, so large, so *intimate*.

I have come to believe that it is the fundamental secret to our success. Without big, bold, in-your-face love, there can be no connection between us and the girls we work with. No sense that we care enough to want to fight to make things different for them. Our love gives them a safe place from which they can explore their world.

In a society saturated in sex, shopping and self-centredness, ironically the one thing that can still truly shock and delight girls is simple, old-fashioned love. I have had people baulk at my frequent use of the word 'love' and look bewildered when girls use it so freely when they are with us. When did love become something to shy away from, and what price will we pay for not being brave enough to openly, unapologetically love our children?

Love is the final, special ingredient that is necessary for the ideas and suggestions in this book to work in the home. To truly connect with your daughter and for *The Butterfly Effect* to be powerful, your approach needs to be based on love. You need to feel something, and invite your daughter to feel something, too. Something more than a desire to be thin, beautiful, popular and hot.

Too often we assume that our daughters know that we love them; that our love for them is instinctive and so needs no explanation. Rather than receiving messages of love from adults, teenage girls often get the message that the rest of the world sees them as hard to handle, troubled, unlovable. The sugar and spice of girlhood turned bad. In popular culture and in adults' conversations, the teen-girl years are often referred to, with a roll of the eyes, as a time that must simply be endured by everyone else. In books, in movies and on TV, teen girls are Queen Bees, Wanna-bees, Bitchfaces, Princesses, Divas, Mean Girls, Drama Queens.

It is time to look at teenage girls through new lenses.

They may be some of these things at times. Yet they are also so much more. They can be hilarious, brave, captivating, creative, intelligent.

When I look at teenage girls, I see:

– The 14-year-old who works at the ice-cream shop near me who always wears pigtails and different novelty hair clips – horses, skulls, ballerinas. Her hair is a source of never-ending surprise and childlike playfulness.

– The 16-year-old who is my friend on Facebook, whose profile page declares her to be a fan of Blu-Tack, Minties, Dory the fish from *Finding Nemo* and Bubble O'Bill ice-creams – and also features her reflections on gender differences and learning Italian.

– The 15-year-old who had a baby, as a result of being raped, and turned up at the school carnival the next week to join in sporting events and cheer on her classmates.

– The 13-year-old who asked me if there was make-up back in my day, too.

– The 14-year-old who sends me copies of her drawings of a fantasy world she has created, and badgers me for contacts in the publishing world as she wants to create her own line of products, 'beginning with a book series and then obviously working my way up to films and merchandising'.

– The 16-year-old who sends me poems she has written on what being beautiful really means and on how she will survive being bullied and emerge a shinier girl.

Try not to let the slammed doors, angry silences or sarcastic asides of adolescence blind you to your daughter's essential *loveableness*. Don't be distracted by the toxic culture our girls are immersed in, for there is a risk that it can blind us to the an even more important reality: the lovablessness of all girls.

Don't be afraid to *show* your daughter you love her.

You can show your love in such simple ways, in everyday moments, just as the parents of these girls have:

When it's really cold and rainy, I come home from school and she's got a cup of hot chocolate and pancakes made for me and my PJs ready to get into. Then we sit under a nice blanket and watch movies all night.

Gemma, 16

My mum writes me little surprise notes and sticks them in my lunch box sometimes. I love them so much, I stick them in my school diary. I've never told her that I look forward to seeing them so much, as she'd probably do it all the time then and somehow that would spoil it. When I feel sad during the day, I look at the letters and smile.

Michelle, 14

I love when me and my mum go shopping together, and after buying many things we will sit in a cafe and just talk. I feel comfortable to talk to her about my life, friends, etc. and it just makes me feel better that I can trust my mum and have that time with her.

Steph, 16

I love it when my mum touches me. That might sound stupid but we're both so busy, we don't touch very often. When we do, it feels like home.

Gemma, 15

You may feel that a good relationship with your daughter is a long way off. If is not working for you both yet, love her anyway, and love *yourself*. And if she seems unlovable at times, remember that is often those who are the hardest to love who need our love the most. Sixteen-year-old Stephanie shared this wisdom with me: 'I don't believe in loving someone because they are perfect . . . I fall in love with people's flaws, because that's what makes them different to everyone else.'

Don't airbrush the issues that may need to be addressed with your daughter; part of loving is setting limits. And don't dwell on the mistakes you both may have made in the past, either.

Just move forwards and fall in love.

Flaws and all.

Appendix 1

Letter To My Teen Self

❦

If you could write a note of advice to your teen-girl self, knowing all that you know now, what would you say to her? I urge mothers to write just such a letter. This exercise encourages reflection on our own lives, creates empathy with our teenage daughters, and affirms the wisdom and strength we have gained.

When you write your letter, remind yourself of how it felt to be a growing girl, alternating (almost hourly) between hope, anxiety, joy, sadness, anger, frustration and pride – so many emotions and often nowhere to put them. Think of all that you have discovered since then and the lessons you can now pass on to the next generation of young women.

When I posted this exercise on my blog, many women shared with me their letters to their teen selves. How touching and insightful they were, such as this one from Melinda:

Dear Teenage Melinda,

You are such a talented person. You could go so far with your clarinet playing and dancing. It doesn't matter if you don't know what you want to do when you leave school, you'll eventually work it out. It's actually not as urgent as everyone says.

I'm very concerned, however, about who you are hanging around with. Yes, they are fun, yes, they are even hilariously fun, but some of them have some major issues. Do you realise how bad some of those issues are? You know the ones I'm talking about. Melinda, you need to see a counsellor about that and so do they. Even though you think you know everything, you are too young to advise them; it is too much for you.

There can be a lot of pressure to have the sort of 'fun' they're having. Do you remember what you said about that? You said to yourself – and to everyone else – that you'd never take drugs and you would wait until you were married to have sex. So why are you associating with people that do these very things? I know you think you are helping them, being a role model, trying to get them to stop. But you can't. As I said, this is too much for you alone.

It was a mistake to get drawn into that way of thinking and acting, Melinda. Just because they seem happy with what they are doing, it doesn't mean they actually ARE.

You don't need a boyfriend. Let me say that again: you actually don't need a boyfriend. Every time you get a boyfriend, it distracts you from being you. And that one boy? Your dad was right; you should have listened to your dad on that one. It might have been annoying to hear, but given that your dad is around 50 years older than yourself, he does know a few things. On that issue, he was spot on.

*Melinda, throw away the **Cosmo** and **Cleo** magazines, they are full of crap. They are a joke. Go and find someone to talk to about your troubles at home.*

One last note: don't stop hugging your dad and telling him you love him. You'll regret it if you don't; he won't be around forever.

With love,

Melinda

ps. You're not fat, you're not fat, you're not fat, you're not fat . . .

I have never met Melinda, but her letter reflects an adolescence that was uncannily like mine. What does that tell us? Teen girls feel similar pressures – to be thin, popular, hot. Many girls feel disconnected from adults who can, and would, help them. Many girls take risks and engage in activities that are self-destructive.

Similarly, this letter by Selena reminded me of some girl-world truths: so often, teen girls rely on others to tell them how valuable they are; and that value is often perceived as depending on sexual desirability.

Dear Teenage Selena,

STOP worrying about what others think of you.

It is NOT compulsory to show lots of flesh. You feel so uncomfortable and self-conscious a lot of the time. Who are you dressing for, anyway?

You do not need a boyfriend. You already know the ones that are no good. Trust your intuition and defeat your need for attention. Get rid of them or say no before anything starts!

It's great that you don't do drugs or binge drink. But stop trying to appear cool by being blasé and knowledgeable about drugs and alcohol. Don't laugh about it. It's not cool or funny. It's stupid and tragic and dangerous. Drug overdoses will kill several people you know.

Your parents love you and they were teenagers, too, once. Listen to them and show your appreciation. Take care of your little sister instead of competing with her. If you stop to think about it, she's actually your closest friend.

Read some stuff on media literacy, body image, sexuality, friendship, etc. Try to understand how the world got to be the way it is. Try to imagine how it could be better. Listen to people's ideas about how it could be better.

Learn about mental health. Do a mental health first aid course. Watch yourself and others for signs of depression and other problems.

Practise being a good friend. Find the girls who have no friends and be a friend to them. Some girls you know are in serious trouble and you don't even notice. Some won't live past 20.

Laugh more. Don't be so serious.

PLAY SPORT or do some exercise!!! It's a gift to yourself for the rest of your life.

And most of all, BE HUMBLE. You're priceless and so is everyone else. You don't know it all (and you never will). But some people know lots of stuff! Most people have something to offer. Accepting criticism is absolutely necessary for personal growth.

Love life!

Selena

What have you learnt? What would you pass on? Write it down. Pass it on.

Appendix 2

Visualisation Exercises

❧

During a visualisation exercise, you relax and go on a guided imaginative journey. The aim is to put your body and mind in a state of calm and control. It is a way of developing controlled breathing and imagination, and of promoting a positive outlook. When we take the time out to be calm and focus on our inner thoughts and our breath, we reinforce the connection between our mind and our body.

Visualisation exercises are not just the domain of the mystical. The effectiveness of visualisation has been well documented. For instance, in the world of professional sport, elite athletes mentally rehearse peak performances;

and cancer patients use visualisation techniques to help regain their health.

I have spoken to many teen girls who have had great success using visualisation activities before bedtime, as part of a ritual to help them unwind and settle for sleep. Often teenagers do not sleep well; in fact, many are considered to be sleep deprived. Developing soothing, positive routines before bed helps them form new sleep patterns.

There are many types of visualisation activities; here I offer two basic guided visualisations for you and your daughter to try. The first is designed to help you face the daily stresses in your lives, such as at school or at work. The second focuses on helping you deal with bullying and intimidation.

I recommend that you or someone else read the visualisation instructions out aloud and make a recording that you can play back regularly to guide you through the exercise. Alternatively, you can have someone read the instructions to you as you do the exercise. The instructions should be read in a slow, soothing voice. The reader should pause regularly, allowing you to focus on what you can see, hear and feel. Calming music or sounds – such as gentle rain or the ocean – may be played in the background. A candle may be lit or essential oils burnt, to create a full sensory experience.

Visualisation exercises are best done in a quiet place where you can completely relax, lying flat on your back with your hands by your side, or sitting comfortably with your shoulders back – not hunched – to allow for deep breathing. Wear loose clothing and make sure that you are comfortable, neither too cold nor too warm.

You may wish to use some of the affirmations spread throughout the previous chapters to create your own visualisation exercises. There are many excellent visualisation and meditation CDs that you may wish to try, too. For younger girls, I like *Indigo Dreaming* by Indigo Kidz, *Butterfly Dreaming* by Denise Allen and *The Rainbow Collection* by Petrea King. For older teens, Denise Allen's *Cool Karma* is excellent and Petrea King has a very good series of CDs suitable for both adults and older girls, which focus on relaxation, self-esteem, forgiveness, improving sleep and more.

About stress

When we dwell on our fears and anxieties, our thoughts have a physical impact on our body. The human nervous system has difficulty distinguishing between a real danger, such as a dog coming to attack us, and an imagined danger, such as a school assignment or work report that is nearly due. If we mentally react to the assignment or report as though it were a dangerous crisis, our body responds by preparing to either fight off the perceived danger or flee from it. This is known as the 'fight or flight' response. There is also actually a third stress response: freezing. We can be quite literally immobilised by our fears and anxieties.

The immediate physical effects of stress include increased heart rate, rapid and shallow breathing, a dry mouth and dilated pupils. Temporary stress can be helpful. It can motivate us to overcome challenges, such as getting that assignment or report in on time. And if we are in fact in physical danger, stress ensures our body responds by virtually shutting down non-essential functions, such as digestion, and becoming tense and ready for action. However, ongoing stress has serious health implications including headaches, disrupted sleep, nightmares, increased or decreased appetite, fatigue and nervous indigestion. One of the most noticeable physical symptoms of stress is tension in your muscles.

Because our minds are not separate from our bodies, there are also behavioural effects of living with ongoing stress, such as inability to concentrate, boredom, loss of willpower, poor time management, overreaction to mistakes, uncontrollable emotional outbursts and the increased consumption of alcohol, tobacco or other drugs.

Perhaps some of your teenager's frustrating behaviour may be a response to her living with stress. Or perhaps you recognise in yourself some of the long-term physical or behavioural responses to stress. Managing stress is something that should be made a priority in your life and your daughter's life. The following visualisation exercise allows you and your daughter to rehearse what it feels like to have the ability and the desire to handle potentially stressful situations with calmness and a positive attitude. Regularly practising this exercise will help you develop new, more positive self-talk so you can respond calmly and optimistically to life's inevitable challenges and setbacks. We cannot always control the events that we experience, but we can control how we respond.

In the first part of the exercise, you will relax your muscles and slow down your breathing, easing the physical symptoms of stress and putting you in a calm frame of mind to begin your visualisation.

Stress visualisation

Gently shut your eyes. Focus only on your breathing. You do not need to change your breathing, just become aware of your breath: in through your nose, and out through your mouth. Long, slow, steady, deep breaths. Feel your chest rise and fall. Listen to the sound of your breath.

Although you will hear other sounds, simply notice them and let them fade from your attention. Focus on the sound of your own breathing. This is your time to relax, to feel good, to be still.

As other thoughts enter your mind, let them pass. Focus only on the present and on your senses.

Visualise the toes on your left foot and imagine each one uncurling. Let go of all tension and feel each toe become soft and relaxed. Allow this feeling to travel along the sole of your foot, to the heel. Now your entire left foot feels relaxed. Every joint is loose. And your breath is slow, long and deep. With each breath you feel more and more relaxed. Calmer.

Focus now on the lower half of your left leg. Feel it sink into the floor, relaxed. Feel this sensation spread up into your knee, which now loosens, and into your thigh. Your whole left leg is warm and relaxed. All you are focused on is your own body and the sound of your breath. You do not allow any other thoughts to disturb your calm. You merely notice them and then let them go.

Bring your awareness to your right foot. Imagine each toe slowly uncurling. Focus on the muscles in your right foot, your lower leg and up into your thigh, until both legs are deeply relaxed.

There is absolutely no tension in your lower body. You feel good. You feel safe.

Soften and release the muscles in your buttocks, too. You feel relaxed and warm.

Now visualise the fingers on your left hand opening. Feel each finger unclench and relax. Imagine each part of your hand softening. Allow this feeling to spread up into your wrist. Feel your hand and wrist loosen. Feel the sensation spread into your elbow. Into your shoulder. Feel your shoulder roll back and drop as you release any tension.

And now visualise this deep relaxation in the fingers of the right hand, the right wrist, the right elbow, the right shoulder.

Both left and right hands and arms are relaxed.

Focus now on your stomach. Feel the muscles in your abdomen soften.

Feel this wave of relaxation spread through your body, into your spine. Allow each vertebra in your spine to loosen. With each breath your body feels more, and still more, relaxed.

Focus now on your neck. Release any tension. Now your face. Feel each line in your brow smoothen. Your lips and teeth gently part as the mouth softens, too. No tightness.

Your whole body is now completely relaxed. And you feel good. And you feel safe and warm.

Breathe.

Now, imagine you have just woken in the morning. The sunlight falls from your window onto your face and fills you with a sense of calm. You feel protected.

The light spreads this warmth from your face right through your entire body. Become aware of being filled with a sense of joy. Bask in this golden, healing light.

Picture yourself getting out of bed and getting ready to go to school / work. You do not rush. You are organised. You are on time. You feel calm and in control.

You feel positive about the day ahead. You know you have all the skills you will need to complete your tasks for the day. You have faith in your abilities.

Take a moment to think about the skills and attributes you have that will ensure you have a successful day. What are you good at? What do you enjoy doing?

Picture yourself leaving for school / work.

Imagine now that you are about to begin a task you usually find difficult and stressful.

You may still feel some stress, but you know these feelings are not necessarily negative. Stress can also be motivating and can encourage you to extend yourself. You have no reason to fear the task before you, because you are prepared. You have set yourself up for success. What preparation did you do so that you can respond differently this time?

Visualise yourself engaged in the task, succeeding at it.

How does it feel to respond calmly and optimistically in this situation?

And as we leave the experience and become focused again on our bodies in the here and now, take a moment to think about what you have learnt from this exercise. Take a deep breath, open your eyes and come back to the present.

You may now wish to write about your observations. How might your life change if you face difficult situations more calmly and optimistically?

About bullying and intimidation

As little girls, many of us were taught to be quiet and compliant, to be 'seen and not heard', to play 'nice'. But passivity can make us vulnerable to being bullied, either in the playground or in the workplace.

Research tells us that most bullies are, despite their intimidating front, often actually weak and insecure and have low self-confidence. That is why they resort to intimidation and violence to get what they want. That is why they pick targets they think are weaker than they are.

I encourage all girls and women to practise standing up for themselves and letting the world know when they are not comfortable and their boundaries are being crossed. This is not about being aggressive. Rather, we all need to be assertive. We need to show – through the words we choose, our tone of voice and our body language – that we expect to be listened to, and to have our opinions heard and respected. When we communicate assertively, we show that we have confidence and inner strength.

It can take years to gain true self-confidence and inner strength, but there is solid evidence that we can speed the process up by practising assertive behaviours, that is, by following the 'fake it till you make it' principle.

When I first started teaching, I worked in a very challenging school. I quickly observed that teachers who showed weakness were completely ignored, or worse still belittled, by the students. Teachers who were aggressive were hated and would often provoke emotional and sometimes physical outbursts from their students, many of whom came from homes where there was violence. These students had been brought up to attack before being attacked.

Although I was at times fearful and worried about gaining control, I knew I had to look as if I was in control and speak with authority. Faking it worked for me in those early days; before I knew it, I was no longer merely pretending I knew how to manage the class. I was managing my class.

The next visualisation activity explores the idea that we can bolster our inner strength by getting in touch with our inner assertive Amazon. Early Greek literature contains many references to strong women, including the Amazons, a race of revered warrior women. In this visualisation you will first imagine your inner Amazon and then picture yourself dealing assertively with a bullying or intimidating person. The aim is to help you develop the strength to be assertive when you face such a situation in real life.

As in the previous visualisation, first you will consciously relax your muscles and slow down your breathing, easing the physical symptoms of stress and putting you in a calm frame of mind, ready to begin.

Bullying and intimidation visualisation

Gently shut your eyes. Focus only on your breathing. You do not need to change your breathing, just become aware of your breath: in through your nose, and out through your mouth. Long, slow, steady, deep breaths. Feel your chest rise and fall. Listen to the sound of your breath.

Although you will hear other sounds, simply notice them and let them fade from your attention. Focus on the sound of your own breathing. This is your time to relax, to feel good, to be still.

As other thoughts enter your mind, let them pass. Focus only on the present and on your senses.

Visualise the toes on your left foot and imagine each one uncurling. Let go of all tension and feel each toe become soft and relaxed. Allow this feeling to travel along the sole of your foot, to the heel. Now your entire left foot feels relaxed. Every joint is loose. And your breath is slow, long and deep. With each breath you feel more and more relaxed. Calmer.

Focus now on the lower half of your left leg. Feel it sink into the floor, relaxed. Feel this sensation spread up into your knee, which now loosens, and into your thigh. Your whole left leg is warm and relaxed. All you are focused on is your own body and the sound of your breath. You do not allow any other thoughts to disturb your calm. You merely notice them and then let them go.

Bring your awareness to your right foot. Imagine each toe slowly uncurling. Focus on the muscles in your right foot, your lower leg and up into your thigh, until both legs are deeply relaxed.

There is absolutely no tension in your lower body. You feel good. You feel safe.

Soften and release the muscles in your buttocks, too. You feel relaxed and warm.

Now visualise the fingers on your left hand opening. Feel each finger unclench and relax. Imagine each part of your hand softening. Allow this feeling to spread up into your wrist. Feel your hand and wrist loosen. Feel the sensation spread into your elbow. Into your shoulder. Feel your shoulder roll back and drop as you release any tension.

And now visualise this deep relaxation in the fingers of the right hand, the right wrist, the right elbow, the right shoulder.

Both left and right hands and arms are relaxed.

Focus now on your stomach. Feel the muscles in your abdomen soften.

Feel this wave of relaxation spread through your body, into your spine. Allow each vertebra in your spine to loosen. With each breath your body feels more, and still more, relaxed.

Focus now on your neck. Release any tension. Now your face. Feel each line in your brow smoothen. Your lips and teeth gently part as the mouth softens, too. No tightness.

Your whole body is now completely relaxed. And you feel good. And you feel safe and warm.

Breathe.

Imagine you are strolling along a beach. The sand is golden; gentle waves are splashing at the shoreline; the sun is warm on your shoulders. The sky is blue and there are white fluffy clouds floating past. You feel safe, warm, happy. Listen to the sound of the waves as they lap against the shore.

You see a woman walking towards you. You know this is your inner Amazon, coming to meet you. You smile as you recognise her. You trust her and feel safe with her.

Your inner Amazon is strong. She can fight to protect you. Yet she is so sure of her own power that she does not even need to exert it. Her mere presence sends a signal that she is a woman to revere.

Your inner Amazon walks tall. Her shoulders are back. She is confident, powerful looking. Look at her closely. What does she look like? What is she wearing? Look into her eyes and see that there is no fear in them.

When she approaches you, she is happy to see you. Imagine how she greets you.

She promises that she will always be with you, that she will defend you and remind you of your own power. For she is you, a special part of you. She will always keep you safe.

Listen to her tone when she speaks. Notice the words she chooses to use.

She reminds you again of your own power and the power of all women. What does she tell you about your own power?

She leads you by the hand to a pool of water. She asks you to look at your reflection. You see that she and you have now merged. You are now the Amazon.

How do you now stand? How do you sound? How do you feel?

You know that you will take care of yourself and keep yourself safe. You know that you have the courage to set boundaries.

Imagine that you now see a person who used to intimidate you coming towards you. Observe their behaviour but choose not to let it upset you. You respond to them calmly and assertively. They are surprised by your new approach and change the way they respond to you.

Listen to how you sound when you talk to them. What words do you use? Observe how you stand.

How does it feel to respond calmly and assertively in this situation?

When I count slowly to three, you will leave the scene, taking with you the feeling of safety, confidence and inner strength.

One . . . two . . . three.

And as we leave the experience and become focused again on our bodies in the here and now, take a moment to think about what you have learnt from this exercise. Take a deep breath, open your eyes and come back to the present.

You may now wish to write about your observations. What might change in your life if you become more assertive?

I adapted the idea of an inner Amazon from the work of Anita Roberts, whose Safeteen program is aimed at eliminating violence in the lives of young people across North America.

Appendix 3

Let's Talk

❦

The following questions are designed to instigate conversation between you and your daughter. If you take turns answering these questions, you may find that you share common ground. Much is made of the differences between mothers and daughters. We often hear young girls complaining that their mothers just don't understand them. Meanwhile, mothers lament that their daughters just don't know what it is like to be in their shoes. It can be enormously healing to share a comforting, connecting moment, when you find yourself thinking, 'Yes, it is the same for me!'

However, our children are not simply smaller versions of

ourselves. These questions will also uncover differences. But different experiences, thoughts and feelings do not need to be reasons for division between you and your daughter; they can be a source of new and deeper understanding. Keep in mind during your discussions that you do not need to reach a consensus; it can be healing simply to connect and explore our different worlds.

Use these questions in whatever way works best for the two of you. It is hard to predict when your daughter will most feel like talking, and too much preparation may make the whole exercise feel fake to her. Grab moments to connect whenever you find them, rather than waiting or planning for the perfect time to talk.

The questions are divided into broad categories so that if there is a particular aspect of your teen's life that is troubling, you can easily find relevant discussion starters. You may wish to choose questions randomly, or even work through the questions from number one to number 50 over a long period of time. Whichever way you approach the questions, always remember that the atmosphere should be fun, loving and supportive.

Communication and connection

1 Describe a time when you were passive rather than voicing how angry or upset you were over the way someone treated you. How could you have handled the situation differently?
2 Describe a time when you spoke before you thought something through. Were there any consequences?

What did you learn for next time?

3 Who is your favourite friend? What qualities does this person possess that make her or him such a valuable friend?

4 Sometimes our friendships need a little TLC. What are five practical ways you can show a friend that he or she is valuable to you?

Inner strength

5 When you were a little girl, who or what were you scared of? Why? How did you overcome this fear?

6 Describe a time when you were pressured by your friends to do something you didn't want to. What was the outcome? How did you feel after giving in?

7 What is your greatest fear? How might you overcome this?

8 What is the bravest thing you have ever done?

9 Where do you feel the safest?

10 Describe a time in your life when you felt as if no one understood what you were feeling. What happened, and what did you do to get through this experience?

Self-esteem

11 What are the things others do that make you feel precious and special?

12 What are the things you do for yourself to feel precious and special?

13 What are you most proud of in your life so far?

14 What are five things that you love about yourself?

Beauty

15 Describe a time when you compared yourself to someone whose looks you admired. How did that comparison make you feel?
16 Who is a woman you admire for reasons other than her looks? What do you like about her?
17 Describe a time when you felt truly beautiful.
18 How do you define the words 'beautiful' and 'ugly'?

Joy

19 When you were a little girl, what made you happy? Why?
20 Describe a time when you laughed, hard and deep.
21 Where is your favourite place to be?
22 What was your favourite book as a little girl?
23 What is your favourite book now?
24 Who is your favourite female character in a book, movie or TV show? What do you like about her?
25 What is your favourite song?
26 Where would you love to go on a trip?

Self-identity

27 When you look in the mirror, what do you see?
28 What is your quote for life?
29 What three words would you like friends and people you meet to use to describe you?
30 What three words would you most like your family members to use to describe you?

Women's status

31 Which commercial brands do you think portray women in a positive light?

32 Describe an advertisement you thought objectified women. How did it make you feel?

33 Flip page by page through a popular fashion magazine. If you had to choose a woman to be within these pages who would you choose to be and why?

34 What qualities do you think it takes to be a powerful woman?

35 What connotations do the following words have for you: 'mother', 'daughter', 'princess', 'queen', 'feminist'?

Reflecting on the past

36 If you could have a day over with someone you have lost, who would it be? Why? What would you do or say?

37 Do you have any regrets in your life so far? What are these?

38 What are you least proud of in your life so far?

39 What can you do in the future to minimise the risk of having regrets or doing things you don't feel proud of?

40 When you were younger, what did you want to be when you grew up?

41 What other sorts of dreams did you have for yourself when you were younger? Have you achieved these? Have your dreams changed as you have matured?

Learning

42 What motivates you when you are learning?
43 How do you like to learn? Do you have a preferred learning style and if so, describe it.
44 What have you learnt from me?

The mother–daughter relationship

45 What is your favourite memory of me?
46 What is your favourite aspect of my personality?
47 If you had only one more day to live, what would you want to tell me about yourself?
48 What do you wish for me?
49 How can I help you to grow and become who you want to become?
50 Can you tell me something about yourself that no one else knows?

Many thanks to my wonderful Enlighten Education team members Jane Higgins, Sonia Lyne and Storm Greenhill Brown for their help in formulating this list.

Appendix 4

Resources

Developing a positive self-esteem and healthy body image

American sites providing media literacy skills needed to combat unhelpful media messages about beauty and body image:

About Face: www.about-face.org

Adios Barbie: www.adiosbarbie.com

Any Body: www.any-body.org

Love Your Body Now Foundation: loveyourbody.nowfoundation.org

Turn Beauty Inside Out: www.tbio.org

American sites offering resources and professional development for teachers wanting to develop media literacy in the classroom:

Centre for Media Literacy: www.medialit.org

My Pop Studio: www.mypopstudio.com

Other useful websites

Enlighten Educationwww.enlighteneducation.com
- My company's website. We deliver in-school workshops for girls on self-esteem, body image, managing friendships, personal safety and career pathways.

The Butterfly Effect: www.enlighteneducation.edublogs.org
- My blog, with weekly posts on all things related to outcomes for girls. Pages particularly worth visiting include the video collection, articles of interest page, and my library.

Girlpower Retouch: http://demo.fb.se/e/girlpower/retouch
- A site that show how easy it is to distort the images we see in magazines and change someone's appearance.

Jean Kilbourne: www.jeankilbourne.com
- Writer and documentary maker who explores the way women and girls are portrayed in advertising.

The Real Hot 100: www.therealhot100.org
- The annual Real Hot 100 list shows that young women are 'hot' for reasons beyond their appearance.

The Beautiful Woman Project: www.beautifulwomenproject.org
- American art project celebrating diversity and real, everyday beauty.

Girl Guiding UK: www.girlguiding.org.uk
- The section 'Girls Shout Out' has some particularly interesting reports on teenage mental health, active citizenship and the pressures girls feel growing up.

Kids Free 2B Kids: www.kf2bk.com
- Australian site that raises awareness about the damage caused by the sexualisation of children and acts to combat this.

Young Media Australia: www.youngmedia.org.au
- Australian organisation with a particular interst in developing media literacy in young people.

Books and magazines for girls

New Moon Girls: American magazine aimed at 8–12-year-old girls. This has web-based activities that accompany it too: http://www.newmoon.com

Indigo 4 Girls: Australian magazine aimed at 10–14-year-old girls. Sells itself as a 'Fun, body-friendly alternative to other magazines on the market, without the airbrushed images, stick thin celebrities and sex articles." http://indigo4girls.com/

Girl Stuff: Your full-on guide to the teen years, Kaz Cooke, Penguin, 2007

Body Talk: A power guide for girls, Elizabeth Reid Boyd and Abigail Bray, Hodder Headline, 2005

The *Girlosophy* series, Anthea Paul, Allen and Unwin

The *Girlforce* series, Nikki Goldstein, ABC Books

Books and magazines for parents and teachers

'Faking It': A special publication that deconstructs the female image in magazines. Available through Women's Forum Australia – www.womensforumaustralia.org

Can't Buy My Love: How advertising changes the way we think and feel, Jean Kilbourne, Free Press, 2000

The Beauty Myth, Naomi Wolf, Vintage, 1993

Perfect Girls, Starving Daughters: The frightening new normalcy of hating your body, Courtney E Martin, Free Press, 2007

Female Chauvinist Pigs: Women and the rise of raunch culture, Ariel Levy, Schwartz Publishing, 2005

Well and Good: How we feel and why it matters, Richard Eckersley, Text Publishing, 2004

Forming and maintaining positive friendships

Websites

Bullying No Way: www.bullyingnoway.com.au
- Australian site that aims to develop and share frameworks for schools that work in eliminating bullying.

Cyberbullying: http://yp.direct.gov.uk/cyberbullying
- 'Laugh at it and you're part of it.' A UK site with solid tips on dealing with cyberbullying and bullying at school.

Books for girls

Respect: A girl's guide to getting respect and dealing when your line is crossed, by Courtney Macavinta and Vander Pluym, Free Spirit Publishing, 2005

Books for parents and teachers

Queen Bees and Wannabes: Helping your daughter survive cliques, gossip, boyfriends, and other realities of adolescence, Rosalind Wiseman, Random House, 2003

Anything She Can Do I Can Do Better: The truth about female competition, Rachael Oakes-Ash, Random House, 2003

Fabulous Friendship Festival: Loving wildly, learning deeply, living fully with our friends, Sark, Three Rivers Press, 2007

Supporting teen girls in crisis

Websites

Better Health: www.betterhealth.vic.gov.au
• Health and medical information for consumers, quality assured by the Victorian government.

Beyondblue: www.beyondblue.org.au
• Australian website on depression

Black Dog Institute: www.blackdoginstitute.org.au
- Australian website on depression.

National Prescribing Service: www.nps.org.au
- Consumer advice on medications; site is funded by the Australian Government Department of Health and Ageing.

Reach Out!: www.reachout.com.au
- Advice targeted to young people, on their mental health and wellbeing

Youthbeyondblue: www.youthbeyondblue.com
- Australian website about young people and depression.

My Body, My Life: www.latrobe.edu.au/psy/projects/body life/index.html
- A free eight-week internet-based group program for 12–18-year-old-girls with a range of body image concerns or unhealthy eating behaviours. The program is part of a research project being undertaken by Hannah Hoile and Professor Susan Paxton from the School of Psychological Science, La Trobe University.

The Butterfly Foundation: www.thebutterflyfoundation.org.au
- Supports Australians with eating disorders.

Suicide Prevention: www.suicidepreventionaust.org
- Public health advocates in suicide and self-harm prevention.

Books for parents and teachers

Adolescent Girls In Crisis: Intervention and hope, Martha Straus, Norton and Company, 2007

My Kid Is Back: Empowering parents to beat anorexia nervosa, June Alexander with Prof. Daniel Le Grange, Melbourne University Press, 2009

I Just Want You To Be Happy, David Bennett, Leanne Rowe and Bruce Tonge, Allen and Unwin, 2009

Making healthy choices around alcohol

Websites

The Facts: www.thesalvos.org.au/need-help/the-facts
- Downloadable report titled 'The Facts: Binge drinking and alcohol abuse'.

A Lot 2 Lose: www.alot2lose.com
- American public service announcements on underage drinking, produced by teen girls.

Alcohol Info: http://www.alcoholinfo.nsw.gov.au
- Offical NSW Government web site on alcohol issues.

What Are You Doing To Yourself?:http://www.whatare youdoingtoyourself.com
- NSW Health site aimed at younger drinkers

My Nite: www.mynite.com.au
- A NSW Police Force initiative offering advice for young people on a range of topics including safe partying.

Books for parents and teachers

Teenagers, Drugs and Alcohol: What your kids really want and need to know about alcohol and drugs, Paul Dillon, Allen and Unwin, 2009

Moving beyond mindless consumerism

Websites

Commercial Free Childhood: www.commercialfreechild-hood.org
- Excellent American site that aims to 'reclaim childhood from corporate marketers'.

Choice: www.choice.com.au
- Australian consumer information.

Phone Choice: www.phonechoice.com.au
- Australian site offering independent, unbiased information on mobile phones and phone plans.

Fair Wear: www.fairwear.org.au
- Australian group committed to working to prevent the exploitation of workers in the clothing industry. Offers some very good resources.

Books for parents and teachers

Branded: The buying and selling of teenagers, Alissa Quart, Perseus Publishing, 2003

No More Frogs To Kiss: 99 ways to give economic power to girls, Joline Godfrey, HarperCollins, 1995

Supporting girls in their learning

Internet safety information and resources for parents, carers and teachers

Think U Know: www.thinkuknow.org.au

Safe Teens: www.safeteens.com

Learning Performance: www.learningperformance.com.au

- A national organisation that runs private sessions developing study skills (N.B. I used to have a financial relationship with this company, but I no longer do. This recommendation is genuine.) There is also a particularly useful series of articles for parents on how they can best support their child during the last few years of school, which is available from this site.

Books for parents and teachers

Real Wired Child: What parents need to know about kids online, Michael Carr-Gregg, Penguin, 2007

Teenage Sleep: Understanding and helping the sleep of 12–20-year-olds, Dorothy Buck, e-book published by the Wellness Promotion Unit, Victoria University, Melbourne, Australia, available at http://eprints.vu.edu.au/467/1/teenagesleep.pdf

Work Smarter Not Harder (Secondary Version), Andrew Fuller, e-book available from his website, www.andrew-fuller.com.au

The Teacher's Toolkit, Paul Ginnis, Crown House Publishing, 2001

The Learning Revolution, Gordon Dryden and Dr Jeannette Vos, Network Educational Press Ltd, 2001

The Mind Map Book, Tony Buzan, BBC Active, 2006

Entering the workforce

Websites

My Future: www.myfuture.edu.au
- Australia's career information service

Australian Job Search: www.jobsearch.gov.au
- Lists current job vacancies

Good Universities Guide: www.gooduniguide.com.au
- Comprehensive information on university education and career options

Year 12 – What Next?: www.year12whatnext.gov.au
- A guide to help Year 12 students plan their post-school education and training.

Bullseye: www.deewr.gov.au/bullseye
- School subjects you like and jobs they can lead to.

Job Juice: www.jobjuice.gov.au
- Useful site aimed at young people – covers everything from choosing a career path to writing resumes

Department of Education, Employment and Work Relations: www.dest.gov.au.
- The 'Parents Talking Career Choices' booklet, available as a free download, is excellent.

Work Place Authority: www.workplaceauthority.gov.au
- Free advice and information on pay and conditions and workplace agreements under the Federal workplace relations system.

Equal Opportunity for Women in the Workplace Authority: www.eowa.gov.au
- Works towards achieving equal opportunity for women in the workplace; has a very good range of educational resources and tools.

Australian Human Rights Commission: www.humanrights.gov.au/sex_discrimination
- Profiles the work lead by Elizabeth Broderick, the Sex Discrimination Commissioner and her Plan of Action Towards Gender Equality.

Books for parents and teachers

Let Your Life Speak: Listening for the voice of vocation, Parker Palmer, Jossey-Bass, 1999

See Jane Lead, Lois P. Frankel, Warner Business Books, 2007

Fire With Fire, Naomi Wolf, Random House, 1993

Closing the Leadership Gap: Why women can and must help rule the world, Marie Wilson, Penguin Books, 2004

Leanne Preston and the Wild Child Story, Leanne Preston, Random House Australia, 2007

General books on parenting girls

What's Happening To Our Girls?, Maggie Hamilton, Penguin, 2008

Growing Great Girls, Ian and Mary Grant, Random House Australia, 2008

Self Esteem For Girls: 100 tips for raising happy and confident children, Elizabeth Hartley-Brewer, Random House, 2000

References

1: Introducing the Butterfly Effect

p. 2   'A quarter of teenage girls surveyed . . .' In fact, 2 per cent of teenage girls surveyed in Australia have already gone under the knife for cosmetic surgery. McLean, T., 'Quarter of teen girls want plastic surgery', AAP, www.news.com.au, 12 August 2007

p. 2   'Among 15-year-old girls . . .' Sixty-eight per cent of 15-year-old females are on a diet. 'Parliamentary Inquiry into issues relating to the development of body image among young people and associated effects on their health and wellbeing: VicHealth Response', www.vichealth.vic.gov.au, September 2004, accessed 14 February 2009

p. 2   'Peer pressure is a cause of pain . . .' Sixty per cent of girls say they have been teased about their appearance. 'GirlForce/Girl World' survey, as cited in Goldstein, N., *GirlForce You*, ABC Books, Sydney, 2006

p. 2   'Seven out of ten teenage girls . . .' Seventy per cent of teenage girls engage in binge drinking and 19 per cent do so on a weekly basis. Healey, Justin (ed.), *Illicit Drugs*, The Spinney Press, Thirroul, NSW, 2004

p. 2   'Pressure at school is also an issue . . .' 'GirlForce/Girl World' survey, as cited in Goldstein, N., *GirlForce You*, ABC Books, Sydney, 2006

p. 2   'As many as one in ten teenage girls self-harm' 'Women

Looking Risky: Body Image and Risk Taking Behaviours',
Commonwealth Office of the Status of Women, http://ofw.
facs.gov.au, 2003, accessed 14 February 2009

p. 2   'Sexually transmitted diseases are . . .' National Survey of
Australian Secondary Students, HIV/AIDS and Sexual Health,
carried out by the Australian Research Centre in Sex, Health
and Society, 2002

p. 2   'In Australia, pregnancy termination . . .' Pratt, A., Biggs,
A., Buckmaster, L. 'How many abortions are there in Australia?'
A discussion of abortion statistics, their limitations, and options
for improved statistical collection. Australian Parliamentary
Library Research Brief no. 9, 14 February 2005

p. 5   'Studies have shown that while . . .' Survey of 1,356 Australian women by The Heat Group, as cited by Byrnes, H.,
'68% of girls think they are not pretty enough', *The Sun-Herald*, 15 May 2005

p. 5   'A 2008 survey found that only one in six . . .' *Australian
Women's Weekly*, April, May, June 2008

2: The Battle Within

p. 21   'We don't need to change our bodies . . .' Wolf, Naomi,
The Beauty Myth, Vintage, London, 1990

p. 23   'Statistics tell the story bluntly . . .' Byrnes, H., '68% of
girls think they are not pretty enough', *The Sun-Herald*, 15
May 2005

p. 23   'A quarter of teenage girls . . .' Byrnes, H., '68% of girls
think they are not pretty enough', *The Sun-Herald*, 15 May 2005

p. 26   'The average person sees around 75 . . .' Young Media
Australia, 'Advertising and Children – is advertising a fair
game for kids?', January 2003

p. 26 'And one in every 11 commercials...' Dittrich, L., 'About-Face Facts on the Media', www.about-face.org

p. 27 'During the last three decades...' Spitzer, Brenda L., Henderson, Katherine A., Zivian, Marilyn T., 'Gender 'Differences in Population Versus Media Body Sizes: A comparison over four decades', *Sex Roles: A Journal of Research*, Vol. 40, 1999

p. 28 'Health experts warn that we are...' 'Overweight and Obesity in Adults, Australia, 2004–05', Australian Bureau of Statistics, www.abs.gov.au, 25 January 2008, accessed 14 February 2009

p. 28 'Large numbers of women and girls..." Byrnes, H., '68% of girls think they are not pretty enough', *The Sun-Herald*, 15 May 2005

p. 28 'Within two years, 95 per cent of people...' Healy, Justin, ed., 'Dieting and Eating Disorders', *Issues in Society*, vol. 235, www.spinneypress.com.au, 2006

p. 29 'Some recent studies have shown...' As discussed by Jenny O'Dea in 'Body Image', STATEing Women's Health Newsletter, Spring 2007, Women's Health Statewide, Children, Youth & Women's Health Service (South Australia)

p. 29 'At least one in five teen girls...' As discussed by Jenny O'Dea in 'Body Image', STATEing Women's Health Newsletter, Spring 2007, Women's Health Statewide, Children, Youth & Women's Health Service (South Australia)

p. 29 'A Victorian study of adolescents...' Patton, G. C., et. al., 'Adolescent Dieting: Healthy weight control or borderline eating disorder?' *Journal of Child Psychology and Psychiatry, and Allied Disciplines*, vol. 38, no. 3, 1997, pp. 299–306, available on Eating Disorders Foundation of Victoria's website, www.eatingdisorders.org.au

p. 29   'A Sydney study of adolescents . . .' O'Dea, J. A. and Abraham, S., 'Food Habits, Body Image and Weight Control Practices of Young Male and Female Adolescents', *Australian Journal of Nutrition & Dietetics*, vol. 53, no. 1, 1996, available on Eating Disorders Foundation of Victoria's website, www.eatingdisorders.org.au

p. 29   'We can be well educated, creative . . .' Martin, Courtney E., *Perfect Girls, Starving Daughters*, Free Press, New York, 2007

p. 33   'British chain Snappy Snaps . . .' Cheesman, Chris, 'Snappy Snaps in "airbrush" boom', www.amateurphotographer.co.uk, 14 August 2007

p. 33   'Many feature the same bee-stung lips . . .' See Van Meter, J., 'About-Face', *New York* magazine, 3 August 2008

p. 34   'Now women shave . . . ' Dr Gary J. Alter, quoted in Navarro, M., 'The Most Private of Makeovers', *The New York Times*, 28 November 2004

p. 35   'You see, as I got older, my body . . .' Salzhauer, Dr M., *My Beautiful Mommy*, Big Tent Publications, 2008

p. 35   'In fact, some studies have shown . . .' Reiss, N. S., 'Women Who Receive Breast Implants More Likely to Commit Suicide', www.mentalhelp.net, 9 August 2007, accessed February 2009

p. 36   'Media expert Professor Catharine Lumby . . .' Catharine Lumby quoted in Tovey, J., 'Teens turn a new page', Life & Style, *The Sydney Morning Herald*, 15 January 2009

p. 37   'An uncommon beauty . . .' French, D., *Dear Fatty*, Random House, London, 2008, p. 84

p. 42   'I don't want the next generation . . .' Kate Winslet, quoted by Henry, L., 'Kate Winslet on Body Image', www.suite101.com, 27 September 2006, accessed 6 February 2009

3: Beyond Generation Bratz

p. 45 'The APA set up a taskforce . . .' The Australian Psychological Society's 'Submission to the Inquiry into the sexualisation of children in the contemporary media environment', April 2008

p. 45 'The Australian Psychological Society is so concerned . . .' 'Helping girls develop a positive self image' tip sheet, The Australian Psychological Society, www.psychology.org.au

p. 47 'When I was flipping through an issue . . .' *Girlpower*, June 2008

p. 50 'In the results of a sex survey in *Dolly* . . .' Of the readers who completed the survey, 53 per cent reportedly said they had given oral sex to a boy. *Dolly*, June 2008

p. 51 'In the 2009 UK television series *The Sex Education Show* . . .' *The Sex Education Show*, Cheetah Television for Channel 4, episode 1, 2009

p. 54 'In fact, research shows that many only participate . . .' *Australian Women's Forum*, submission to the National Council to Reduce Violence Against Women and Children, 2008

p. 54 'An extreme example would be . . .' Cobb, M., 'Ambivalent Sexism and Misogynistic Rap Music: Does Exposure to Eminem Increase Sexism?', *Journal of Applied Social Psychology*, vol. 37, 2008

p. 55 'The American Academy of Pediatrics . . .' These comments were made by Dr Michael Rich, spokesperson for the American Academy of Pediatrics Media Matters campaign.

p. 56 'A British study found that watching video clips . . .' Bell, B. T., Lawton, R., Dittmar, H. 'The impact of thin models in music videos on adolescent girls' body dissatisfaction', *Body Image*, 2007

p. 58 'The inquiry was prompted by . . .' Rush, E. and La Nauze, A., 'Corporate Paedophilia: Sexualisation of children in Australia', Discussion paper number 90, The Australia Institute, October 2006

p. 59 'It would be a mistake to . . .' Parliament of Australia, 'Sexualisation of children in the contemporary media', Senate report, 26 June 2008

p. 59 'Clive Hamilton, the former Director of the Australia Institute . . .' Hamilton, C., 'Sexualisation Inquiry: How adland had its way', www.crikey.com.au, 27 June 2008

p. 59 'Catharine Lumby, from the University of . . .' Cleary, S. (producer), 'Little Women', *60 Minutes*, Channel 9, 22 June 2008

p. 60 'No sensible person would argue . . .' Eckersley, R., *Well and Good: Morality, meaning and happiness*, Text Publishing, Melbourne, 2004, p. 130

p. 62 'Amanda Gordon, President of the Australian Psychological Society . . .', Amanda Gordon, quoted in 'Letting Kids Be Kids', *Today Tonight*, Channel 7, 29 March 2007

p. 63 'Recent British research indicates that parents . . .' The Senate Standing Committee on Environment, Communications and the Arts, 'Sexualisation of Children in the Contemporary Media', Commonwealth of Australia, 2008

4: Planet Girlfriend: The Highest Highs, the Lowest Lows

p. 72 'The lyrics (that I knew for definite) . . .' 'Big Girls', Buckfield, Linda Mary / The Electric Pandas

p. 79 'A study by a group of Australian academics . . .' 'Teens subjected to mobile phone bullying', Drennan, J., Brown, M., and Sullivan-Mort, G. 'M-bullying and mobile communication: Impacts on self-esteem and well-being.' Unpublished working paper, January 2008

p. 79 'A similar study claimed . . .' Results of a study of more than 700 students conducted by the Australian Catholic University.

p. 80 'Teenagers' brains "are all tuned up . . ."' Fuller, A. 'Into the Mystery of the Adolescent Mind', *Byron Child*, no. 16, December 2005–February 2006

p. 85 'They are based on the respect rules . . .' Macavint, Courtney and Vander Plimyn, Andrea, *Respect: a girl's guide to getting respect and dealing when your line is crossed*, Free Spirit Press, Minneapolis, 2005

5: Drinks with the Girls

p. 95 'For a long time we thought [tobacco] was something . . .' Patton, Professor George, Centre for Adolescent Health, Melbourne, as reported in Harford, Sonia, 'Girls Gone Wild', *The Age*, 22 May 2008

p. 95 'Studies reveal that girls aged 12 to 15 . . .' Cited by Harrison, D., and Gordon, J., 'Booze blitz: alcopop tax lifted by 70%', *The Age*, 27 April 2008

p. 95 'Over 80 per cent of the drinking done by children . . .' Healey, Justin (ed.), 'Alcohol Abuse', *Issues in Society*, volume 252, www.spinneypress.com.au, 2007

p. 98 'In 2008, Australian consumer group Choice . . .' 'Alcopops', www.choice.com.au, February 2008

p. 101 'What every girl should know about alcohol' All facts and statistics in this section are sourced from 'Women's Health' on the Australian Government's website www.therightmix.gov.au

p. 103 'Concerned by the way adults in the community . . .' Page,

Robyn, Lovett, Judy and Risbey, Sonya, 'Rethinking the drinking', St Peter's Collegiate Girl's School, Adelaide, July 2005

p. 104 'Research shows that teenagers who drink excessively . . .' As reported by Morse, J., 'Women on a Binge', *Time*, vol. 159, no. 13, April 2002

p. 105 'As Jennifer Duncan reported . . .' Duncan, Jennifer, 'Binge drinking, much more than a youth issue', *The Sunday Mail*, 22 June 2008

p. 109 'Contrary to popular belief, taking a stand . . .' Based on Harrison, 'Booze blitz: alcopop tax lifted by 70%', *The Age*, 27 April 2008

6: Shopping for labels . . . or love?

p. 112 'The current generation of children . . .' Bachmann Achenreiner, G., & Roedder John, D., 'The meaning of brand names to children: A developmental investigation', *Journal of Consumer Psychology*, vol. 13, no. 3, 2003, quoted in 'Materialism, and Family Stress' fact sheet, Commercial Free Childhood, www.commercialfreechildhood.org

p. 112 'The average teenager in the United States . . .' Heim, K., 'Teen talk is, like, totally branded', *Brandweek*, 6 August 2007, quoted in 'Materialism, and Family Stress' fact sheet, Commercial Free Childhood, www.commercialfreechildhood.org

p. 112 'In the UK, almost half of children . . .' Nairn, A., Ormrod, J., & Bottomley, P., 'Watching, wanting and well-being: exploring the links', National Consumer Council, London, 2007, quoted in 'Materialism and Family Stress' fact sheet, Commercial Free Childhood, www.commercialfreechildhood.org

p. 113 'In Australia, children aged 10 to 17 . . .' Statistics compiled in YouthSCAN 2007, by Quantum Market Research, reported in 'YouthSCAN 2007', NSW Office of Fair Trading, Reviews and Reports, www.fairtrading.nsw.gov.au

p. 113 'Australian teens are working and earning more . . .' Statistics compiled in YouthSCAN 2007, by Quantum Market Research, reported in 'YouthSCAN 2007', NSW Office of Fair Trading, Reviews and Reports, www.fairtrading.nsw.gov.au

p. 113 'Researchers have even found . . .' Schor, J., *Born to Buy*, Scribner, New York, 2004, quoted in 'Materialism, and Family Stress' fact sheet, Commercial Free Childhood, www.commercialfreechildhood.org

p. 114 'Kids are the most powerful sector . . .' Quoted in Quart, A., *Branded: The buying and selling of teenagers*, Perseus Publishing, New York, 2003

p. 117 'Australian cosmetics guru Napoleon Perdis . . .' www.napoleonperdis.com

p. 117 'As Jennifer Thomson writes, '"Girl Power" is . . .' Thomson, J., 'Girl Power', www.thefword.org.uk, 5 April 2008

p. 119 'While many teenagers are branded . . .' Quart, A., *Branded: The buying and selling of teenagers*, Perseus Publishing, New York, 2003

p. 120 'The national franchise director of . . .' Quoted in Marcus, C., 'Frock Therapy in a Crisis', *The Sydney Morning Herald*, 26 October 2008

p. 120 'That kids feel products make a contribution . . .' Center for a New American Dream, 'Thanks to ads, kids won't take no, no, no, no, no, no, no, no, no for an answer', www.newdream.org, 2002

p. 122 'As Alissa Quart writes . . .' Quart, Alissa, *Branded: The buying and selling of teenagers*, Perseus Publishing, New York, 2003

p. 122 'Now it's all about "the 'image'..." 'Consumers and Designer Brands', a global Nielsen report, April 2008

p. 128 'Almost 10 per cent of people who went bankrupt...' Australian Government Insolvency and Trust Service Australia, 'Profiles of Debtors 2007', www.itsa.gov.au, 23 September 2008

p. 128 'The highest stress level is among those...' Statistics compiled in YouthSCAN 2007, by Quantum Market Research, reported in 'YouthSCAN 2007', NSW Office of Fair Trading, Reviews and Reports, www.fairtrading.nsw.gov.au

p. 128 'A spokeswoman for the New South Wales...' 'Mobile phones "bankrupting" more teens', *The Sydney Morning Herald*, 7 November 2007

p. 131 'You may remember the story of...' 'Teen sends 14,500 texts in a month', news.ninemsn.com.au, 12 January 2009

p. 136 'What I really want that money can't buy...' Winning entry in the 'What I really want that money can't buy' contest, Center for a New American Dream, www.newdream.org

7: Rage and Despair: Girls in Crisis

p. 137 'Helping adolescent girls in crisis...' Straus, M. B., *Adolescent Girls in Crisis*, W. W. Norton & Company, New York, 2007

p. 139 'Respected therapist and author Martha B. Straus...' Straus, M. B., *Adolescent Girls in Crisis*, W. W. Norton & Company, New York, 2007

p. 143 'The suicide risk of a person with an eating disorder...' Statistic appears in 'Myths and Stereotypes', Eating Disorders Foundation Incorporated, www.edf.org.au

p. 143 'One study showed that 96 per cent . . .' Wilson, J. L., et. al., 'Surfing for Thinness: A pilot study of pro-eating disorder web site usage in adolescents with eating disorders', *Pediatrics*, vol. 118, no. 6, December 2006

p. 143 'Another study showed that these sites . . .' Bardone-Cone, A. M., Cass, K. M., 'What does viewing a pro-anorexia website do? An experimental examination of website exposure and moderating effects', *International Journal of Eating Disorders*, vol. 40, no. 6, 2007

p. 143 'Yet the biggest risk factor . . .' According to the New South Wales Eating Disorders Foundation, 'Frequent and extreme dieting is the biggest risk factor in the development of an eating disorder,' in 'Myths and Stereotypes', Eating Disorders Foundation Incorporated, www.edf.org.au

p. 148 'Right now, between 2 and 5 per cent . . .' 'What is depression?', Youthbeyondblue, www.youthbeyondblue.com

p. 149 'And personality may play a role . . .' 'Causes of depression', Black Dog Institute, www.blackdoginstitute.org.au, accessed 23 January 2009

p. 150 'If you feel that for a period of two weeks . . .' Based on 'Understanding Depression', beyondblue, www.beyondblue.org.au

p. 152 'The highest rate of suicide in females . . .' Based on the most recent figures available in January 2009, 'Causes of Death, Australia, 2006', Australian Bureau of Statistics, www.abs.gov.au

p. 155 'In fact, four out of five young people . . .' 'Youth suicide prevention – the warning signs', www.betterhealth.vic.gov.au

p. 158 'Heroin, cocaine and ecstasy are used by fewer . . .' 'Teenagers and Substance Abuse', www.healthfirst.net.au, an ACT

Government initiative for the people of the Australian Capital Territory and surrounding region

p. 158 'Amphetamines such as speed and crystal meth . . .' 'Teenagers and Substance Abuse', www.healthfirst.net.au, an ACT Government initiative for the people of the Australian Capital Territory and surrounding region

p. 158 'On the other hand, 25 in every hundred . . .' 'Teenagers and Substance Abuse', www.healthfirst.net.au, an ACT Government initiative for the people of the Australian Capital Territory and surrounding region

p. 158 'But to put the risk in perspective . . .' 'Australian Social Trends, 2008: Risk taking by young people', Australian Bureau of Statistics, www.abs.gov.au, 23 July 2008

p. 159 'The statistics also show that . . .' Figures in this paragraph are based on '2007 National Drug Strategy Household Survey: First results', Australian Institute of Health and Welfare, www.aihw.gov.au, 27 April 2008

p. 159 'We know that adolescent brains . . .' Associate Professor Michael Baigent, quoted in 'Tackling teen drug use', beyondblue, www.beyondblue.org.au, 28 May 2007

p. 160 'Society can create a certain amount . . .' Clive Skene, quoted in 'Tackling teen drug use', beyondblue, www.beyondblue.org.au, 28 May 2007

p. 162 'When she's at a loss for words . . .' Straus, M. B., *Adolescent Girls in Crisis*, W. W. Norton & Company, New York, 2007

p. 162 'When girls can be angry . . .' Straus, M. B., *Adolescent Girls in Crisis*, W. W. Norton & Company, New York, 2007

8: Schooling for Life

p. 167 'Yet teens spend only 15 per cent . . .' As cited by Fuller, A. 'Into the mystery of the adolescent mind', *Byron Child*, December 2005 – Feb 2006

p. 168 '[T]hose who work in and for schools . . .' Whitby, G., 'Pedagogies for the 21st century, having the courage to see freshly', a paper delivered at the Australian Council of Educational Leaders annual conference, 2007

p. 171 'From sports psychology, we know that the best coaches . . .' Hartley-Brewer, E., *Self Esteem for Girls, 100 Tips for Raising Happy and Confident Children*, Random House, London, 2000

p. 172 'In Australia, girls are more likely than boys . . .' Statistics in this paragraph are based on 'Girls and ICT, what the research tells us', Department of Education and Training, www.schools.nsw.edu.au

p. 172 'Rather than trying to find ways . . .' Williams, B. T., 'Girl power in a digital world: considering the complexity of gender, literacy, and technology', *Journal of Adolescent & Adult Literacy*, vol. 50, no. 4, 2007

p. 176 'Consultant psychologist Dr Judith Paphazy . . .' Dr Judith Paphazy quoted in Milburn, C., 'Cotton-wool kids must burst bubble', *The Age*, 3 October 2005

p. 181 'I keep telling Dad I need a bigger monitor . . .' Thomas, A., *Youth Online: Identity and literacy in the digital age*, Peter Lang Publishing, 2007, as cited in Williams, B. T., 'Tomorrow Will Not Be Like Today: Literacy and Identity in a world of multiliteracies'. *Journal of Adolescent & Adult Literacy*, 51(8), May, 2008

9: Career Girl

p. 197 'On average, the weekly pay a woman . . .' 'Average Weekly Earnings, Australia, 2007', Australian Bureau of Statistics, reported in 'Generation f: attract, engage, retain', Equal Opportunity for Women in the Workplace Agency, www.eowa. gov.au, 2008

p. 197 'The imbalance is right there from the beginning . . .' *GradStats*, Graduate Careers Australia, no. 12, December 2007, reported in 'Generation f: attract, engage, retain', EOWA, www.eowa.gov.au, 2008

p. 197 'That pattern is carried through . . .' 'EOWA Census of ASX200 Companies: Gender distribution of income for top earners', EOWA, 2006, reported in 'Generation f: attract, engage, retain', www.eowa.gov.au, 2008

p. 197 'Out of all 200 companies that make up . . .' 'EOWA Australian Census of Women in Leadership', EOWA, 2006, reported in 'Generation f: attract, engage, retain', www.eowa. gov.au, 2008

p. 197 'Finally, and unsurprisingly, women . . .' According to a 2002 study by the Human Rights and Equality Opportunity Commission, 86 per cent of reported incidents of sexual harassment involved a female victim and a male perpetrator. 'Sexual Harassment: A bad business. Review of sexual harassment in employment complaints 2002', HREOC, 2003, reported in 'Generation f: attract, engage, retain', EOWA, www.eowa.gov. au, 2008

p. 199 'The federal government's Equal Opportunity for Women in the Workplace Agency . . . ' 'Generation f: attract, engage, retain', EOWA, www.eowa.gov.au, 2008

p. 200 'One survey showed that almost 70 per cent . . .' Barclay,

R. G., et. al., 'Fitting Fathers into Families: Men and the fatherhood role in contemporary Australia', Department of Family and Community Services, 1999, quoted in 'Generation f: Attract, engage, retain', EOWA, www.eowa.gov.au, 2008

p. 200 'Another found that 60 per cent . . .' 'Striking the balance: Women, men, work and family', Sex Discrimination Unit, HREOC, 2005, quoted in 'Generation f: attract, engage, retain', EOWA, www.eowa.gov.au, 2008

p. 201 'Women with partners spend almost 30 hours each week . . .' Headey, B., et. al., 'Families, Incomes and Jobs: A statistical report of the HILDA survey', Melbourne Institute of Applied Economic and Social Research, The University of Melbourne, 2006, quoted in 'Generation f: attract, engage, retain', EOWA, www.eowa.gov.au, 2008

p. 201 'While the professional and legal positions . . .' Maguire, E. *Princesses and Pornstars*, Text Publishing, Melbourne, 2005

p. 202 'Employers that mistakenly avoid recruiting women . . .' 'Generation f: attract, engage, retain' Equal Opportunity for Women in the Workplace Agency, www.eowa.gov.au, 2008

p. 205 'Deborah Rhode, an expert on gender equality . . .' Rhode, D. *Speaking of Sex: The denial of gender inequality*, Harvard University Press, Cambridge, Massachusetts, 1997

p. 205 'There is nothing enlightening about shrinking . . .' Williamson, M., *A Return to Love*, HarperCollins, New York, 1992

p. 208 'I insisted we have a structured program . . .' Freedman, M., 'Once upon a time, there was a banana', Mia Freedman blog, www.mamamia.com.au, 27 April 2008

p. 210 'Most teenagers can find only part-time work . . .' The

unemployment rate for 15–24-year-olds is 2.8 times higher than that of 25–64-year-olds: 'How Young People are Faring '08', The Foundation for Young Australians, www.dsf.org.au, 2008
p. 215 'Young people wanting to start their own . . .' Preston, L., *Leanne Preston and the Wild Child Story*, Random House Australia, Sydney, 2007

Every effort has been made to acknowledge and contact the copyright holders for permission to reproduce material contained in this book. Any copyright holders who have been inadvertently omitted from acknowledgements and credits should contact the publisher; omissions will be rectified in subsequent editions.

Permission to quote material from the following sources is gratefully acknowledged:

Mia Freedman, www.mamamia.com.au. Reprinted with permission.
Elizabeth Hartley-Brewer, *Self Esteem for Girls: 100 Tips For Raising Happy and Confident Children*, published by Vermilion. Reprinted by permission of The Random House Group Ltd.
Dannielle Miller and Melinda Tankard Reist, 'The Grinches who Steal Innocence', *The Sydney Morning Herald*, 4 January 2008.
Martha B. Strauss, *Adolescent Girls in Crisis*, W.W. Norton & Company, New York, 2007. Reprinted with permission.
Winning entry in the 'What I really want that money can't buy' contest, © Center for a New American Dream. Used with permission. All rights reserved.

Acknowledgements

My sincere thanks go to the following people, for whom I am tremendously grateful.

In my day-to-day work:
All the teenage girls I have worked with. You shine so brightly that at times I am almost blinded by your magnificence. Love and light to you all.

The schools that allow me the privilege of working with their girls.

Francesca Kaoutal, my Yellow Brick Road partner who always says 'yes' and always makes me laugh.

Sonia Lyne, Jane Higgins, Storm Greenhill-Brown, Dianne Illingworth Wilcox, Kelly Valder, Nikki Dingle, Nikki Davis, Melinda Nielsen, Monica Lamanta, Kellie Mackareth and Christine Elias – my Enlighten Amazons who have not only shared the dream but helped it grow larger and more vivid.

In my writing:
Margaret Gee, my literary agent, who set the wheels in motion.

At Random House, Katie Stackhouse, for a supportive introduction, and Roberta Ivers, Nikki Christer, Jessica Dettmann and the rest of the team, for the follow-through.

Vanessa Mickan – my divine editor, who has made this whole process such an absolute joy.

The principals, teachers, parents and specialists who allowed me to interview them for this book. It is richer for your contributions.

All the teenage girls who agreed for me to interview them. I feel so honoured that you allowed me in and cared enough to just keep talking until I *got it*.

Those who reviewed chapters for me and offered constructive, meaningful feedback: Dr Michel Beale, Melinda Tankard Reist, Julie Gale, Jane Higgins and Dr Brent Waters.

Associate Professor David Benet, who not only reviewed chapters but also provided a thoughtful, passionate foreword. I am deeply humbled.

In my life:
My husband, Wayne, for understanding that my work will also always be one of my greatest loves and for being man enough to encourage me to just get on with it.

My children, Teyah and Kye, for not only accepting my work but sharing my love for it, too.

My au pair, 'Suzy McCool', who helped me with the children over the school holidays so I could devote more time to writing. Just like Mary Poppins, you are 'practically perfect in every way'.

My mother, Lorraine, sister, Chantelle, and extended family the Waters, Davises, Fletchers and Millers – for your practical support and encouragement.

All my girlfriends, who have understood that I am often too busy writing to come and play.